Becoming a Dad:
How Fatherhood Changes Men

by
Bruce Linton, Ph.D

Fathers' Forum Press
Berkeley, Ca
USA
www.fathersforum.com

Fathers' Forum Press
1521-A Shattuck Ave. Suite 201
Berkeley, Ca 94709
USA
510-644-0300
www.fathersforum.com

© Bruce Linton 2012

ISBN-13: 978-1468067545
ISBN-10: 1468067540

Book and cover design: Brad Reynolds: www.integralartandstudies.com
Text font: Garamond Pro, 11 pt.

In memory of my father Hyman E. Linton (1910-2001)

"When you teach your child, you teach your children's children"
The Talmud

Thank you to my home team…
Carolyn Sweeney, Phyllis Greene and Natalie York.

"We must let go of the life we have planned,
so as to accept the one that is waiting for us."
—Joseph Campbell

Dedicated to the next generation of fathers:
Morgan Linton, Michael Straws, Joshua Linton, Benjamin Antin,
Michael O'Krent, Noah Linton, Brian Sweeney, Evan Mironov

To all of the dads who have participated in the Fathers' Forum I will
be eternally grateful. It has been my honor to have shared in your lives
at such an important time. Much of this book reflects the inspiration I
received from our many meetings.

To the many colleagues, friends, and family who have always been
interested and supportive of my work with dads…
thank you to one and all!

Special appreciation is due to Andrew Samuels, Arthur Coleman
and Robert Bly who have shaped my vision of
what is possible for a man and a father.

Thank you Gayle Peterson, Ph.D. for your support of my work and vision.

Thank you to Hugh Cook for editorial help and encouragement.

Julia and Mike, Morgan and Daina….the best kids a dad could have!
I am a lucky man.

Table of Contents

Poems:

Surrender

I have given up all hope of enlightenment.
Working hard
loving my wife,
caring for my children,
that is enough for me.

Preface

I did not write this book. The essays here were inspired by the twenty-five years of groups I have been leading for new and expectant fathers. I was just lucky enough to jot the moment down and develop the ideas. I now encounter in the streets of Berkeley, California some of the "pioneering" fathers who were in my groups in the 1980s and struggled along with me making sense and meaning out of becoming a father.

And I am glad to report that we were right—history and time have borne us out! Being a father is truly one of the most worthwhile, creative, and meaningful relationship we can experience in our lives. It was these men who, like the millions of loving and nurturing fathers that are actively involved with their children and are largely ignored by the media, are re¬defining what it means to be a man. The media instead will search for the deadbeat dad or child abuser, and run an hour-long special on a sick and mentally disturbed man who tormented his children.

Today there are millions of kind, and caring dads developing as parents, being inspired by their role as a father and participating right from the birth of their baby's life.

The development of this new paradigm for fatherhood—the involved and active dad—will be our most significant contribution in this millennium. Yes, the microchip and the incredible technological advances we will see in our lives will be spectacular. The advances in the biological sciences will improve the health and longevity of our children in so many ways. I believe the infrastructure of all this will be our families and the new role fathers have engaged in within the family. This will be the "terra firma" of our new socially networked world that is developing all these new technologies.

So if you are a father, you know that the meaning of our lives as men is deeply rooted in our experiences with our children and all our struggles with loving and nurturing them.

Remember we are all part of the great community of fatherhood. Each of us as men has unique insight into how caring for our children has changed us as men—and is changing the world!

Ways to Use This Book

This is not a "how-to" book. It is intended to stimulate your thinking about what it means to be a dad and what value you place on being a father and parent in your own life.

I hope you might share this book with your wife, partner and friends, and that the essays will encourage further discussions while enhancing your experience of fatherhood.

Here are some ways to "use" this book:

- Expectant dads and newly "born" fathers—as well as dads with young children—will find this book helpful in developing a personal understanding of the challenges and tensions we encounter as fathers and parents.

- Couples will benefit as well, allowing mothers especially to catch a glimpse of the transitions and struggles that fathers experience.

- Fathers' groups and men's groups will be able to use these essays to stimulate discussions and explore their experiences as fathers and men.

- Childbirth and parent educators will find the themes reflected in these essays useful as resource material and as a way of getting students to think about the tensions fathers face in becoming parents.

- Obstetricians, pediatricians and family practice physicians will find this book helpful in introducing the dads they encounter to the normal anxieties men experience when they become fathers.

Son

33 years of looking
and still, such blindness--
my son of three
points
to the small berries
on the bush
I have walked by
everyday
unnoticed

Becoming a Father: Men and Friendship

My father used to play with my brother and me in the yard. Mother would come out and say, "You're tearing up the grass." "We're not raising grass," Dad would reply. "We're raising boys." —Harmon Killebrew

I cannot remember, in my childhood or adolescence, ever thinking about being a father. I didn't think about it, in fact, until my late twenties, when my partner of three years asked if we should have a baby. She says that was the only time she ever brought up a subject I did not want to talk about. No other subject we have ever discussed (moving, changing jobs, buying a house) made me feel so ambivalent.

I was twenty-nine years old my wife, twenty-five, and it seemed an appropriate time to begin a family. We had both grown up in families of four children. I had recently become licensed as a marriage and family therapist in California. She was a registered nurse at our local hospital, and at that time she was working in the nursery. What more could I ask for: a wife who was a nursery nurse!

Although I didn't know it at the time, this was the beginning of my journey to the understanding that by becoming a father I would learn about being a man. I was very confused inside. I found myself faced with what I knew to be one of the most important decisions in my life, and in terrible conflict. How I had been taught to be a man—decisive and in control—went against everything I was feeling inside. How I was taught to be as a man and what I was feeling inside seemed completely opposite. The uncertain and ambivalent feelings that I was taught to suppress and resist in order to be a man were just too strong to be denied. Looking back thirty years, I can now understand that, even before our child had been conceived, something was changing within me.

Typically, I began to explore my decision to become a father by making lists. How would our lives be changed by a child? My lists of positives and negatives grew daily. Finally I became aware that this decision would have to be made with insufficient information. I would have to take a leap of faith. I would need to trust something, as yet unknown, inside myself.

I would need to trust that I could live with fear of the unknown. Fear of not really knowing how our child would change my wife, our marriage, or me. Fear of the emotional and financial responsibilities. Fear that we would not have a healthy baby. Fear of a life that was out of my control. I can now reflect back to this time and appreciate how I was coming to know myself as a man — how control and certainty, traits I had long identified with the "masculine," were merely a facade, a defense against the feelings I was having. I now know those sleepless nights of anxiety about fatherhood were the beginning of learning how to understand my own fear and self-doubts. Rita and I took the decision to have a baby seriously. We went away on weekends and questioned and fantasized about life would with a child would be like. What would it be like to be a family? We eventually both came to an important realization. We had hoped to do some traveling as part of our relationship, perhaps extended trips to Europe, China or Nepal. Through our discussions, we came to realize that by having a baby we would not be able to indulge ourselves in traveling the way we had planned. We came to understand that by having a baby we would be doing another type of traveling, an inner journey. We would make discoveries about who we were as parents. At this point, having a child began to feel like an adventure. The hope of pregnancy was transformed into a gift: the miracle of being able to have a baby.

In April 1981 our son Morgan was born. As I held him in my arms in the days that followed his birth, I would often cry. How vulnerable and fragile he seemed. How this little baby would need me! I felt overwhelmed. Was I ready to care for and love this baby? Was I prepared for this most precious of trusts, to nurture a child? How strongly attached to him I felt. How lost I felt about what I was to do as a father.

I was up with him one night when he was about a week old—it was probably about 2 am—and I had turned the radio on. As the announcer read the news, I recall being profoundly concerned about the state of affairs in the world. The world needed to be a safe, welcoming place for my son. War, poverty, crime—these problems needed to be solved . . . immediately!

My son, one week old, was already bringing me into contact with the world in a new way. New feelings of concern and compassion were being born within me. Since he was born, my interest in the environment, schools, the economy and public safety has grown intensely alive within me. It was as if my personal sense of isolation were coming to an end and a new feeling for community beginning to develop.

I was proud and excited to become a dad, but I also felt overwhelmed and bewildered about my life. My wife and I talked about our experiences together, but something was missing for me. I began to realize that she had many women friends with whom she could talk about what it was like to be a mother. I discovered that I had no men friends with whom I could talk and share my feelings about being a father.

I had the realization that what I needed was to talk with other fathers. I needed to hear from other dads how they were coping with all the changes in their lives and relationships.

This has been one of the most important insight for me as a father: I need to be with other fathers. This insight led me to help form a group for new fathers. The impact of this small group of men took me out of my isolation and also helped me have a forum for the feelings I was either trying or longing to express to my wife. Here in this group of men I had a home for all my confusion and bewilderment about myself as a new father. Here was a place for me to come and understand myself as a father—and as a man.

For further self-reflection and discussion:

1. Who are your two closest male friends?

2. What efforts do you make to keep in contact with your friends?

3. As a father and a parent, what is important for you to share with another friend/father?

When A Man Gives Up

When a man gives up
the world of things
and is no longer driven
by profit
his day is done;
he welcomes the night knowing
it is dark with secret things
and the good fortune for his children,
that their father has left home
to search for something deeper that
is hidden
inside.
If his children understand this journey
their father has taken
they will rejoice
and they will not have to go so far away
to find what is most precious
inside themselves.

Finding Time for Fatherhood

The guys who fear becoming fathers don't understand that fathering is not something perfect men do, but something that perfects the man. The end product of child raising is not the child but the parent. —Frank Pittman

It has been most difficult to find the time to write this essay! When our two children were little, it was obvious why it was impossible to get much private time. Day-to-day tasks were like digging a hole in the sand on the beach: no matter what size the hole, the water would fill it up. The demands of being both physically and emotionally present for infants and young children is pretty much full-time work for both parents.

Now that our children are older (12 and 16), I am surprised that parenting responsibilities are still a major focus of our everyday lives. With each year of fatherhood, I have had to ask myself, "What kind of father do my children need now?" I have been lucky in that my personal interests and professional career have been interwoven. I have focused on coaching and counseling parents with young children on how to balance parenting with both working at jobs and careers. This is an issue I constantly struggle with myself, and I am not always satisfied with the results.

Time is our most valuable resource as parents, our most precious commodity. Think about it. We work all our lives so we can retire—so we can do what we want with our time—and the way we define or spend our time defines who we are and what we value.

Our society sets values on the way we use time that have always offended me. In the United States, you can receive a tax credit if you work and place your children in childcare. If you stay at home with your children, however, or work part-time, there is no tax credit. What we say in the U.S. is that we value only the time you spend working. It sends a strong message that parenting is not a priority.

We do not need to be locked in a battle between time spent working and time spent parenting. Both work time and family time sustain us in very important ways, and we gain unique satisfactions from both. There are practical matters to consider as well: we need money to live, yet our children are little for such a short time. How will we prioritize our choices?

How we choose to prioritize our time as fathers is very difficult. There is still an unspoken assumption in our society linking our identity as men with our work. Although this is changing, careers still provide men with more esteem, status and financial reward than does the time they spend parenting. Also, it is still accepted that the money a man makes is the way he supports his family.

Most of the expectant and new fathers I work with are terribly conflicted by wanting to spend time with their young children while having to cope with the financial pressures. When both parents work, dads as well as moms want more time with their young children. I think we have a much larger social problem than we are aware of in terms of the emotional cost for both parents and young children when it comes to the use of time in the early years of parenthood.

Being a father is now more central to our identity as men, but this is causing problems and repercussions in the work world. Many employers stigmatize new dads, assuming they are less committed to their work than men who don't have children. An attitude that men are less capable if they need to take time off for school activities or medical visits can discriminate against the working dad.

What I think is happening is not that men value work less, but that fatherhood is becoming equally important. While work was once the only source of meaning for a man, fatherhood and parenting have become as important to his self-esteem as his work.

This development parallels the progress that women have made during the last 25 years, with an interesting twist. While women have expanded their identity beyond the role of motherhood—exploring the possibilities of new roles in modern society—men are exploring new possibilities and larger roles within the family. They seek the potential to be more emotionally and physically available to their children. As women have moved increasingly into the world of work, men desire to play a bigger role in the world at home.

As dads we need to examine our desires and expectations. If we are socialized to believe self-worth is dominated by our relationship to careers, then we have a conflict when we become fathers and find ourselves wanting to be part of our children's lives. More and more men are choosing to be fathers, and making the necessary financial sacrifices to be involved in family life will require a change in the "culture of work." We need to find ways to be nurturing and involved fathers while making important contributions in the workplace.

From my perspective as a family therapist, it is easy to see that the changes couples and babies go through in the first year of the baby's life depend on having the necessary time to form the attachments that normally occur. Yet we do little as a society to protect this time for parents or children. Pressures mount quickly for parents to get back to work. I am not saying that every couple should stay home with their new baby. What I am proposing is that, especially in the early years, there is a need for flexibility in regards to time so that fathers, mothers and babies can have enough time to get to know each other. It takes time to come to a personal understanding of what parenthood and family life mean for each of us as individuals.

In some ways the public problem we have—that we don't provide enough support for families—must be resolved in a private way. Each of us, as a parent and as part of a couple, needs to find the way to create the work–family balance that can sustain our families emotionally as well as financially. We as fathers need to support each other in parenthood. We dads must give each other the encouragement to take risks both emotionally and financially in order to be more integrated in our families.

In choosing our priorities we make sacrifices, but the sacrifice is easy if we recognize the gain. Fathers are being sold a bill of goods whenever we are told that our work will give us the entire fulfillment we need in life. We are now discovering that we need to feel connected with our children and families in order to be truly content. No father on his deathbed has ever said, "I wish I had spent more time at work."

We are coming to understand as fathers that our relationships with the important people in our lives—especially our children—are of paramount importance to feeling good about ourselves and feeling that our lives have meaning.

When I asked my children what they think makes a good parent, they gave me the following responses: Our 12-year-old daughter said that taking your kids to school and picking them up (on time), as well as having time to play with them and help them with their homework, was important. She also commented that young children should spend more time with the parents than with a baby sitter.

Our 16-year-old son summed it up by saying that it just takes time to spend with your kids. He said people should not be prejudiced against teenage fathers—that if they have the time to spend with their kids, they can be good fathers too. It all comes down to time.

I know from the dads and new parents I work with that balancing our many needs and desires while finding the time can often be overwhelming. The same is true for my wife and me. I encourage you not to give up the struggle, however. Finding time for your children is extremely important, because it will not only benefit their development but, particularly for us fathers, make all the difference in how we feel about what is of real value and meaning in life.

Like the seasons of the year, our lives as parents—as fathers—go through transitions. Look at the time you spend with your children in relationship to the season of their lives. Getting your son or daughter off to a good start often takes more time and is very intense. I can't remember how many times I've heard, "They are little for only such a short time." I can't remember any days (or nights) that were longer than when our son and daughter were between birth and two years old. Today I can already feel they have one foot out of our house and the other into lives of their own, and I could not be prouder of each of them. Our life has been wonderful as well as difficult, but more than a few times I have wished we could go back in time and my children could be our babies once again.

Eight Important Considerations for Fathers:

1. From birth onward your physical presence is important to your child. Understand how "being there" for your children often means saying little but standing in the audience, sitting in the bleachers or driving the carpool.

2. Listen, listen, listen and listen to everything your children want to tell you. As they get older take seriously their positions, ideas and opinions.

3. Whether married or divorced, work with your partner for your child's well-being. When differences arise, as they will, try and work things out thinking about the example you are setting for your children.

4. At whatever age, stage or phase your children are at, play with them. Learn to be part of their world of play based on their interest. Whether playing dolls, collecting baseball cards, reading a novel or a comic book, watching TV, going on walks, riding bikes, building sand castles—allow yourself to be led by your child in the joy of playing together.

5. As your children grow, learn about their friends and their families. Try to build bridges with your children's friends' families.

6. Try (knowing you will make mistakes—and be kind to yourself) to live a life that shows your child that hope and opportunity and possibilities exist for them in their lives. Your life is an example of this optimism about life.

7. When it is in the best interest of your child, say no. Trust that although your children may not always feel positively toward you, know you are doing what is in their best interest. This is the most difficult aspect of fatherhood.

8. Try to keep a sense of humor. There are many opportunities to become depressed as the pressures of life increase as your child grows up. Be conscious of your attitude. Is life a burden or a challenge for you? Consider how this affects your children.

For further self-reflection and discussion:

1. How did your father balance work and family life?

2. How have your routines changed once you had a child? (Or, if you are expecting a baby, how will your routines change?)

3. Can you have different priorities at different times in life?

My Father

Father there and not there
wanted more for his children
introvert, shy, tough
courageous
lost at times
both confused and certain
loyal and hardworking
tentative Jew
optimist, thoughtful, narrow-minded
dogmatic
curious and capable of change
educated without college
investor, speculator, entrepreneur
small businessman
loved vacations and loved to dance
dedicated to his wife
nothing more important than his children
(his one true treasure...us)
liked to exercise
always improving himself
never stopped growing
core belief: "you can always find a way to work it
out...
every day is chance for satisfaction and happiness"
just a man
and so much more

Who Was Your Father...Who Are You?

What was silent in the father speaks in the son, and often I found in the son the unveiled secret of the father. —Friedrich Nietzsche

When men become fathers, they are confronted with a profound challenge to understand what "father" means to them. Most men are perplexed by this. In both my personal and professional lives, I have searched to understand why becoming a father is such an uncertain experience for today's men.

In the fathers' groups I have led, most men look to their own fathers as examples of how to be parents. Reflecting on their own fathers' behavior often leaves them feeling sad, lonely, frustrated, angry and ambivalent. In our group, together, we struggle to understand and make peace with our fathers. Many of the men in my groups feel very limited by having a father who was either physically or emotionally absent from their lives. We try to understand how we can be more available and more emotionally connected with our families. Some of the men who had abusive fathers become fearful and wonder if they might hurt their own children. If we must rely on our own personal fathers as teachers or mentors on parenting, we may feel limited. To understand himself as a man, each of us must come to an understanding of his own father and his father's influence on his life, both positive and negative.

However, I question the limitation of understanding one's own father as a path to becoming a more nurturing parent. We have to look beyond our fathers. Where must we look to gain a broader perspective about what it means to be a father?

The idea of an original model after which similar things are patterned—a kind of prototype—is what the depth-psychologist Carl Jung called an archetype. I thought there would have to be a prototype for what it means to be a father, but I was surprised by what I discovered.

There is an archetype for motherhood. The "Madonna and Child" image appears in some form throughout the world. The biological basis of pregnancy and giving birth sets up a relationship between mother and child that is, to varying degrees, stable in all parts of the world. This is not the case for fatherhood. Images of fathers and their relationships with their children and families are not stable, and vary widely from culture to culture. If this is true, what does it tell us about the meaning of fatherhood?

To begin with, it seems to indicate that fatherhood is socially constructed. Depending upon the culture, the historical time and the needs of the society, fathers may play a variety of roles. It is both a frightening and liberating thought that fathers have no prototypic model for how to be parents. This means that men can stop looking towards (and perhaps blaming) their own fathers for instruction (or lack thereof) on how to be fathers. They can begin to explore within themselves and in the world at large for the kinds of behavior and family life they would like to provide for their own children. They must turn to each other, father to father, and learn together how to develop positive nurturing relationships with their children.

Understanding what it means to be a father is a very personal journey for each and every one of us. Each father, in his own way, must search out and discover what kind of father he wants to be for his children. It is a difficult journey and many men shy away from questioning what it means to be a father. For those who are willing to take the journey, however, it is surely a path filled with heartfelt expectations. Hopefully it is a path shared with fellow fathers where, at this time in history, we can help each other along the way. Perhaps never before have we fathers had such an opportunity to consciously participate in the lives of our children.

It's a great time to be a father. Seize the moment!

For Further self-reflection and discussion:

1. What was most difficult for your father in his life?

2. How did your father fail you in your life, and how was he there for you?

3. If you were to write a letter to your father about how you feel about   him, what would it say?

Kosher

a few words said over the making of wine
or meat or bread
does not make it kosher.
If that were the case
we could pronounce a few good words
to change the world.
We must work hard through our actions
to sanctify life.
Everyday we must practice kindness,
thoughtfulness, patience in all
our acts.
Caring for children,
tending the earth,
understanding our relationships with others.
To be truly kosher, we must not
affirm the things that insult our soul,
whether in words, deeds or song.
And so when my wife
lifts a glass of wine
on the Sabbath,
she sanctifies it
in the most ancient of ways,
by bringing the reverence
she gives
to life.

Fathers and Marriage

Marriage is a promise. Not just between the couple but to the community at large, to generations past and to those yet to be born. —Anonymous

The most important things in life are not things—our relationships are! The relationship that has had the most impact on our own lives is the one we had with our parents. By the same token, our relationship with our partners—our marriages—will influence our children in many profound ways.

Providing good schools, living in a decent neighborhood, participating in community and sports activities, having a computer, offering music lessons—these are some of the ways we help to nurture our kids as they grow and develop. Every father wants his child to grow up to be an honest and caring person. But how does that happen?

If we reflect on our own parents' marriage, what was it like? Did they treat each other with dignity and respect? Were they considerate and understanding with each other? How did they handle the inevitable anger and frustration that comes not just with parenting, but with life? Did they seem to enjoy being married? Why did they have children?

Marriage and fatherhood are relationships that force us to reflect on the family in which we grew up. As children, we absorb much of what goes on around us. We usually are unaware of what or how or when the events and relationships from our past may influence the choices and relationships we are having now.

Much of the work of dynamic psychotherapy is to help individuals become aware of the long-forgotten, now unconscious responses we have to the relationships and events happening now in our lives.

Thinking about our parents' responses in their marriages can go a long way in helping us understand not only how we may respond to our partners but also what value and meaning marriage offers us. And luckily for us today, more than ever, we can work with our partners to create the marriage that we want. We can evolve beyond the restricted structures and social constraints that may have limited our parents' ability to find a more satisfying relationship within their marriage.

But most important for us as a father is to understand that by caring for and loving our wives we can be offering a great gift to our children. Letting our child see our concern and interest in our partner tells them much about what human relations are based on. And when difficulties do arise, being able to bear the tension and disappointment allows us to stay in the relationship emotionally even when we may not be feeling positive about our spouse. Think about that…that we can love someone and at the same time feel disappointed by him or her. How we encounter and work in our marriage lays the ground for what a potentially loving relationship may mean for our children. The relationship between husband and wife is the center of a child's developing morality. How he treats himself and others grows out of the observations he makes of the way his parents treat each other.

Many men who become fathers today take pride in their involvement, right from birth, in the nurturing and caring of their infants. This is a very positive change in our culture. Fathers' involvement in active parenting is creating a new model for family life.

I am always struck by meeting fathers who are so positively engaged with and excited about their children, but appear so uninterested in or disengaged from their relationships with their wives. I often comment to couples whom I see in my psychotherapy practice that they act like single parents who are living together. Everything in their relationship seems to focus on their child.

In many cases, as time goes on, the parents begin to work out many of their interpersonal difficulties through their children. Young children may begin to wonder why their parents seem to have so much love for them and not seem to care much about each other. What does an experience like that teach a child about interpersonal relationships?

And sometimes marriages need to change. At times, for specific reasons, a couple finds out they are not able to work out their differences. Most couples with children try to go the extra mile to make their families work, but it is not always possible. Sometimes the interpersonal issues from our family of origin are just too mismatched with our partner's character, and no matter how hard the two people try they cannot resolve the tension and frustration they feel with each other. If they can value their roles as parents, then they can make the transitions that are necessary not only to separate or divorce, but also to keep the parenting support their children need to survive and thrive. Some marriages are just not sustainable. It is no shame or cause for blame if a marriage can't be maintained. We can try to provide our children with the example of two sincere and loving people who are trying to work at life's challenges, while still considering the children's best interests.

There is a great renaissance today for men, and today's father is the cornerstone. A new developing sense of masculinity and gender identity is unfolding around the development of the nurturing father. It is important, rewarding and valuable to participate in the care giving of our children. But if we don't also nurture our marriage, what have we really conveyed to our children about being a loving and caring person? One of the greatest gifts a father can give his children is to love his wife. This is a lovely statement, but in reality it is a difficult and often lifelong adventure to understanding your spouse.

For further self-reflection and discussion:

1. What is most difficult for you about loving another person?

2. What are the trade-offs in being married? (What do you find liberating about being married, or in a committed relationship, and what is restricting?)

3. What do you like most and least about being married?

Life Boat

When my daughter
on her six-year-old legs

runs down the street
after her brother
& gets on the back of his skateboard

and his arms like oars
push them down the street

just for a second
the meaning of things
is perfectly clear!

Preparing for the Birth of Your Baby

It sometimes happens, even in the best of families, that a baby is born. This is not necessarily cause for alarm. The important thing is to keep your wits about you and borrow some money. —Elinor Goulding Smith

Becoming a father and a parent is a transformational process for a man. When a man becomes a father, he comes in contact with a deep paternal masculinity through loving his child, partner and family. When a child enters a man's life, a new depth of feeling and emotion is awakened within him. Growing up male in the United States is for many men an education in how to deny their feelings. From an early age we are taught not to cry, not to feel dependent, and to be in "control" of our emotions.

When we begin to approach fatherhood either by beginning to talk about having a child with our partners, or by hearing those life-changing words, "Honey, I'm pregnant," an emotional avalanche of feelings begins. It is this avalanche of new feelings, which if understood and not feared, can help humanize us as men in the most fundamental and profound way. When we begin the journey toward fatherhood we have the opportunity to recover the nurturing, patient, dependent and tender side of our own personalities that was, for many of us, socialized out of us as we made our way toward adulthood. Becoming a father is our chance to become a man who is truly masculine by being emotionally available for our children and our wife.

In my work with fathers, what I hear new dads talk about most is their interest in being participating and active parents. They want to be able to nurture their child and family by being more than just the breadwinner—which is all that many of their fathers were. They don't want to just put bread on the table for their families, they want to sit down and eat dinner with them too!

A new universe of feelings is awakened in a man through the process of pregnancy and birth. It has been my experience that, although women often appreciate this new awakening of feeling in their spouse or partner, they don't really understand what it means to the new or expectant father.

Men's involvement in pregnancy and birth, and their participation in the early years of their children's lives, has changed dramatically over the past 25 years. In 1965, about 5% of fathers attended the birth of a child. In 1989, almost 95% of fathers were present. Men are clearly asking for more participation in the childbirth process. It is also interesting and encouraging to note that, according to a recent survey on men and work, 75% of the men would accept slower career advancement if they could have a job that would let them arrange their work schedule to have more time with their families. At the prospect of becoming a father, men are filled with excitement, fear, wonder, worry, love, and confusion. (To name just a few feelings!) Throughout the pregnancy and birth, the man now becoming a father is trying to find ways to express and integrate these and many more feelings. Since most prenatal classes focus on the woman's experience in pregnancy, dads often feel that this potpourri of new feelings they are experiencing is a sign that something may be wrong with them! Not true. It is normal to feel overwhelmed and insecure about the impending life-changing event of having a child. Worries about finance, time, and how a baby will change your relationship with your partner are all normal concerns of "healthy pregnant father."

In recent years, prenatal education has made an effort to understand the fathers' experience during pregnancy and birth. Many programs are now offering classes for dads based on the model that I developed through the Fathers' Forum programs. The key factor for us as men is to be able to talk with other expectant and new dads about their experiences in this life-changing time. So even if your prenatal classes don't offer opportunities for you to meet with the dads alone, ask a few of the men in your classes if you can spend some time together and talk about your experiences of the pregnancy and what the birth may be like. Many men begin during the pregnancy itself to develop bonds with their children. Expectant fathers in my groups have talked about how they enjoyed laying their hands on their partners' bellies and talking to their babies. This very personal and private communication is very powerful as a prenatal bonding ritual. Helping choose the birth attendants, midwife or doctor, and being included in the choice of where the baby will be born are other ways men begin to get involved.

In my work with fathers, I see men seeking to understand the journey from man to father, and I see how something very special happens when this search for understanding is shared with other men/fathers. Finding a relationship with other men/fathers during pregnancy is an important way in which we can help initiate each other into fatherhood. Seeking out male friends or family members who are willing to share with you their stories of how their life has changed since they have become a father is a way not only to prepare yourself for parenthood, it may also help you to begin thinking about the way you will want to be a father.

Men today want to participate in the birth process, and in most cases are expected to share the birth of their child with their wife. They want to be there right from the start to welcome their baby into the world. They want to be involved in offering support and love, and to share this most intimate part of life with their wife.

I wonder what it will be like for the next generation of children whose fathers attended their births—when our sons and daughters say to us that they are thinking about having a baby, and we can say, "I remember when you were born." And we can tell them what it meant for us to be present at their birth.

Fathers who are able to participate in the birth of their children often report that the sharing of this experience with their wife remains one of the most important moments in their lives. Even—or especially—if the birth is difficult, or a cesarean delivery, men feel strongly about being present at this special time. Sharing the birth experience together for many couples, the intensity and emotionality of the birth, can deepen their bond as a couple as they share one of life's most intimate experiences together.

Expectant fathers also need to explore what they need at the birth. What kind of support does the expectant dad need? Many of the new fathers I have worked with talked about how important it was to have a male friend, or other father, with whom they could talk. Beginning to consider which friends and family could be there to understand and appreciate what your feelings are can be very helpful. Thinking about sharing your experiences with someone other than your wife can help. Sometimes new dads are reluctant to share their fears and worries with their wives because they feel it would be upsetting for her. In wanting to protect their wives from being "hurt" by their worries, dads often neglect these feelings as burdensome or inappropriate. It is best to seek out male friends and other dads to share your fears and negative feelings. We all have them. If it is not comfortable or doesn't feel right to talk with your wife about them, don't let them go unexpressed. Most dads I have worked with felt much more connected to the pregnancy and birth once they were able to acknowledge the negative feelings that they experienced. And most found that other new and expectant fathers were very interested in hearing about them.

"Engrossment" is the term researchers use to describe the father's total absorption and preoccupation with the presence of a newborn. This term could be expanded to describe the early weeks of family life. The first few hours after the delivery are a very important time for the new family to be together. The bonding triangle of mother, father, and baby is configured by all being together in these first moments of family life.

The most important aspect of family bonding for new fathers is time. If the new father can have the time to be with his partner and child, the natural process of bonding will take place. There is nothing the father needs to do but spend the time with his new family. As fathers get to know their newborns, they often find that a new level of feeling is awakened in them.

This too is an especially important time to be with and talk to other fathers about your experience. It can deepen your own experience, as well as validate your growing sense of what being a father is all about. It is important not to be isolated as a new father, and to have other resources than your partner to share the many changes new fathers go through. Being in a fathers' group is one way to find affiliation with other men.

A father is looking for a psychologically satisfying place within his family. There are many benefits to his involvement in pregnancy, birth, and the early years of a child's life. These benefits are not only for his child and wife/partner but also for his own understanding of what it is to be man and a father. What I have seen in my work with fathers is that we, as fathers, need to share our experience and support each other. Our dialogue as a community of men helps us understand and appreciate the most important and dynamic life transition: becoming a father.

For further self-reflection and discussion:

1. What training, classes or other preparation did you have for becoming a father?

2. Can you find two other expectant or experienced fathers to meet with, and find out how they feel or felt about the pregnancy of their partners and the birth of their children?

3. After reading this chapter, what would be the one question you would like to ask another father about pregnancy or birth?

The Meaning of Things

There must be a small opening
between the making lunches,
driving and picking up the kids from school,
tending the laundry, groceries,
monthly bills needing to be paid,
phone calls to return,
letters to be written,
grass to mow,
weeding and planting,
coaching the baseball team
practicing guitar,
reading a little and
going to work...

There must be a moment
when the inner world
and the outer world
overlap
and for a moment
the dishes that need to be washed
are so much more than just a chore
but an offering to God...
well, anyway
my wife always feels better when
the kitchen is clean

How Having a Baby Changes a Couple's Relationship

It's not only children who grow. Parents do too. As much as we watch to see what our children do with their lives, they are watching us to see what we do with ours. I can't tell my children to reach for the sun. All I can do is reach for it, myself.
—Joyce Maynard

When a man and a woman have a baby, it is a profound transition— the most important change in their adult lives. How becoming parents can affect them as individuals and as a couple is still not well understood in our culture. Of all the Western industrialized countries, the United States offers the least support for family adjustment and development. Politicians would like us to believe that we put a priority on family life, but the reality is just not so. How a man makes the transition to parenthood, and how a baby changes a man's relation to his wife, are very important areas for us as men to understand.

When a baby is born, the focus of the new mother's attention is on the baby. This is part of the normal developmental process. Mothers become preoccupied with the baby's needs, often to the exclusion of everyone and everything else. This is part of her biological makeup. Most new fathers are unaware of this normal maternal preoccupation and are often surprised and frustrated at how abandoned they may feel. We have no information about what to expect after a baby is born. Men have very little preparation for this intimate part of life. Childbirth preparation classes often help us share with our wives the experience of pregnancy, but we are unaware of what to expect emotionally after the baby arrives. So what's a dad to do?

As a new father feels the emotional withdrawal of his wife's attention, he can take comfort in knowing that her total attentiveness to their baby is normal. He can begin to notice whether he has feelings of anger and hurt. Often the time after birth may stimulate unconscious feelings that remind the father of his own childhood. But what about his normal needs for attention and intimacy?

Intellectually, a father can become aware that he is participating in an intimate, common and normal experience of the biological foundation of life. He can take comfort in knowing that as their baby adjusts to being outside rather than inside its mother, this intense connection needs to sustain itself for a while.

He can also be active in sharing and bonding with his wife and baby by participating in this great mystery of getting to know himself and his wife in their new roles as parents, and becoming acquainted with this new being called their child. He can begin to get a glimpse of his own vulnerability as the uncertainty of his new role and relationships emerges.

Often the new feelings a man discovers when he becomes a father press him to overwork, perhaps to drink more or to have an affair—all of them ways of trying to escape from the pain of feelings he may be having about the change in relationship with his wife. Even when he is aware of the biological calling for his wife's intense intimacy with the baby, he still feels his own intimate needs neglected.

What I found in my research on new fathers is that throughout history men have had other men—other fathers—with whom to share the transition to parenthood. The joy and loneliness, the fear and confusion were emotions men were able to experience with each other. This was a natural intimacy that men had between them. It is something we have lost in Western industrial countries. Historically, we have always had a community of male friends to turn to at the critical times in our lives. Without this important relationship in a man's life, all his intimacy needs, especially for understanding and comfort, are demanded of his wife and his marriage.

The stereotype of men persists that "they don't share their feelings." What I have found in my work and research is that men don't have opportunities to share their feelings. In my fathers' groups and my all-day workshops we never seem to have enough time to talk, discuss and share all that we want to. The fathers comment on how, unlike their wives—who have many groups available—they have no place to go to specifically talk about the changes they are going through as men and dads.

Not only do we need to be able to establish an intimate relationship with a group of men when we become fathers, but throughout our lives we need the companionship, intimacy and support we can offer each other. Building and maintaining relationships is not easy with the pace and mobility of life today. For us as men to value our male friends, and to work on developing our relationships with each other, takes commitment. Finding ways to create opportunities to be together to talk about the important experiences we are living is of immeasurable value. Having a community of male friends can profoundly affect the quality of our marriages and how our children feel about us as fathers and men. Maybe the loneliness we feel after our babies are born is not just the change in the relationship with our wives, but the sadness we feel at being without any close men to share this most important time in our life.

For further self-reflection and discussion:

1. How has your relationship with your partner changed since you became parents?

2. Do you feel jealous of your partner's relationship with your child?

3. How do you imagine other couples are affected by becoming parents? Do you think, as men, we have any similar experiences as we become fathers?

Muddling Through

I am not an investment banker
or a corporate visionary.
I am not building a house
or jack hammering cement.
I am not a long haul truck driver,
a highly paid lawyer, or an anesthesiologist:
all honorable professions.
I am out walking,
noticing the box elder,
the wild Cyprus tree in our neighbor's yard,
the dahlias, deep purple ones, on the planting
strip near the street.
I know the terror and joy that
each day brings;
any moment darkness can descend,
cancer can find you, a child becomes ill,
someone blows up,
your heart skips to many beats,
a plane crashes; a flood washes away
your house and family.
I have taught my children to look for
the beauty of the moment.
I practice this
today.
So many of my days
I muddle through
somewhere between
fear and contentment,
searching, searching
for the beauty of the moment
to remind me
of the sensation
that there is a meaning
to all that is.

Sex and Parenthood

Parenthood: That state of being better chaperoned than you were before marriage. — *Marcelene Cox*

Having a baby and making the transition to parenthood is a very complicated process. I say this from both my professional perspective as a family counselor and my own experience as a father of a 10- and 14-year-old. With all the various pressures on young families, there is often not enough time or energy for parents to have the sexual contact one or both partners desire. As I look back on my marriage (and it's still true today), both my wife and I have had to discuss and accommodate our personal needs and desires, as well as the logistics of work schedules and kids' schedules, to find the time and "timing" to be together sexually.

Before we had kids, which seems like another lifetime now, our sexual relationship was fairly spontaneous. We had time together most evenings, and we were young and had less complicated professional and emotional commitments. Over the years together, just being parents has changed our emotional dispositions, our bodies and our desires for sex. After eighteen years together, we are truly different people than we were when we first met. Our sexual relationship has in its frequency and intensity been rather unpredictable. I have tried to keep an open dialogue about how I feel about our sexual relationship, but at times it has been difficult to discuss. I think each of us has been concerned about hurting the other in discussing our sexual need. My wife and I continue today to struggle with our sexual desires and our needs for intimacy while we try to understand our individual differences, what we need in terms of sex, and how to feel close and connected in our marriage.

How important is sex to a marriage? Sex seems to be the emotional barometer for most marriages. Not in the sense that the more sex the better the marriage, but in the sense that the way couples can discuss openly and with concern for each other their feelings about intimacy is a good index of the health of their relationship.

In this way, sexuality is a symbolic way each partner becomes emotionally vulnerable. As a psychotherapist, I am acutely aware that each individual's ability to be emotionally vulnerable is often more a reflection of the influences of the family he or she grew up in than of feelings about a current relationship or spouse.

I find in my work that in the couple's relationship, the individuals are working out the intimacy (or lack of it) that they experience in their own family of origin. Although couples will focus the tension in their relationship on sexuality, that is often a reflection of feelings of being appreciated and understood. What psychotherapists call "being seen" by one's partner—a sense that the other person understands or empathizes with your experience, separate from his or her own—appears to be a significant building block for emotional intimacy. As my clients report to me, there is a high correlation between this type of being seen and sexual intimacy and desire.

In working with fathers I have noticed a few particular themes in regard to sexuality. Some men have difficulty adjusting to the change in their wife's body shape after the birth of a baby. With all the advertising and media hype about how women's bodies should look, the whole Playboy image can create problems for men (and women). Fathers often need to free themselves from the fantasies of the commercialism of women's sexuality to appreciate the reality of their wife's sexuality. During pregnancy, some men begin to resent the attention their wives get. They can develop an underlying anger that can become a powerful inhibitor to feelings of sexuality. After the baby is born the two-person bond is shifted. A new father often feels excluded by his wife's attention to their newborn. This can lead to feelings of anger, sadness, and depression. Oftentimes these feelings are expressed by either emotional or physical withdrawal. Many men (and women, too) aren't consciously aware of these feelings. It can be difficult to talk about these feelings, even if the parents are aware of them. Especially in the early years, when most fathers are trying to find their place in their families, they may feel it would be a burden on the relationship to discuss the way they feel. They may even feel guilty for having these feelings.

Some men feel uncomfortable about having sex during pregnancy. They have fears they will be hurting the baby or their partners. Many men need to look at how they view their own bodies in relationship to a pregnancy. If, during the pregnancy (this can also be true throughout the marriage), a man's partner agrees to accommodate his physical needs but isn't interested herself in lovemaking, how should he feel? If he is enjoying himself and she isn't, should he feel guilty? Is this kind of sexuality OK?

Is sex necessary? For some couples, it is critical to have an active sex life. It serves as both a physical and emotional outlet for tension. For other couples, the fun and excitement they experience through sex is very important. While many couples need to have sexual intercourse to feel satisfied, other couples find cuddling and holding will suffice. At various times in a relationship, couples feel the need to put their sexuality on hold while they are working through other issues in their life or relationship.

There are many legitimate forms of lovemaking that we overlook. Stress and tension in life are often relieved by feelings of closeness and by holding and touching another human being (most often our partners). Kissing, massage and mutual masturbation are all ways to fulfill physical desires we all normally need to express.

Through working with the sexuality in our marriages we learn about so many things: our need for closeness and intimacy, our own desires and our own bodies. By discussing these feelings with our partners we gain perspective and develop emotional maturity. We learn that our sexual desires and needs can be a doorway to a deeper understanding of our partners and ourselves.

For further self-reflection and discussion:

1. How has the sexuality in your relationship changed since you had a child?

2. Do you know other dads or men with whom you can talk about your sexual feelings in your marriage?

3. How important to you is the sexual relationship in your marriage?

Morning Meditation

We could be rushing off to school, but
we slow the moment down and
I consider what is really of value
to me.
I make my decision.
and with such mastery she adjusts her socks,
folding over the tops,
slips on her tennis shoes and ties her laces
with her total attention
and then
comes the big decision for the day:
double knots?

From Man to Dad:
How Fatherhood Changes Men

No man can possibly know what life means, what the world means, until he has a child and loves it. And then the whole universe changes and nothing will ever again seem exactly as it seemed before. —L. Hearn

The most profound and complicated event in a man's life is becoming a father. It is also the least understood and, until recently, the least researched topic in the study of adult development. No life transition—not getting married, changing jobs, moving, or completing educational goals—will have as long-lasting an effect on a man's sense of purpose as becoming a parent.

When I first became a father 30 years ago, I thought I was prepared for fatherhood. I had completed my training as a Family Therapist and was well educated in the stages of the family lifecycle. But I was not prepared for the deep and powerful reorganization of my identity that I would experience. While the changes in my outer world—our daily routines, work schedules, the disorganization in our house, the big changes in the time my wife and I spent together—were very apparent, the feelings going on within me remained mysterious and confusing. It was during our pregnancy, at the birth, and the very intense first year of parenting that I began to try to understand what was happening to me as I was becoming a father. It became apparent to me how little information or preparation is available on what it would be like for me to become a father. In retrospect, I realize how helpful it would have been to have a better understanding of this important transition in my life.

In our lives today, the major risk factors of pregnancy and birth are not medical. The real risk factor is that the necessary time for the emotional development for both parents and the baby—individually and as a family—will be short-circuited. The father, mother, and baby will not get the opportunity to experience the first year together to adjust and learn about their new relationships and roles. Father will be off to work in a week or two, mother will need to return to work after a few months, and the baby will end up in "really good daycare."

Here in the United States we tend to focus on the physical experiences both during pregnancy and birth and in the postpartum period. Discussions about lack of sleep, the baby's feeding schedule, food preparation, and when and whose relatives will be visiting become the focus of many new parents' early experiences. We are often out of touch or ignore our own inner experiences. Most of us have grown up in families where sharing our feelings was often minimized. In times of stress or change we have been taught in our families not to talk about our feelings but to hold them inside and be stoic. This is particularly true for us as men. In the weeks following the birth of our son Morgan in 1981, I found myself feeling bewildered and overwhelmed. As I talked with my wife about my feelings I felt something was missing for me. She was very supportive and caring about what I had to say about being a dad, but still I felt I needed more. I realized that she had many women friends with whom she could talk about being a mother. I found that I was lacking male friends who were fathers who I could talk to about being a dad. I realized that what I wanted, what I needed, was to talk in confidence with other fathers about what I was experiencing. I needed to hear from other fathers how they were managing with all the changes in their lives brought about by having a baby.

From this searching for a more intimate connection with other men to discuss feelings about fatherhood I organized a one-day workshop for expectant and new fathers called the "Fathers' Forum." In fliers that I sent out and posted around my town (Berkeley, California) I described the workshop as follows: "The Fathers' Forum will present a one-day workshop for expectant and new fathers, as well as men who are considering becoming a parent. This is an opportunity for us as men to meet together and explore what it means to become a father. We live in a society/culture that promotes competition and isolation among men. Rarely do men find time to discuss their inner reflections, ambivalence and doubts with each other. This workshop is an opportunity to have a dialogue with a community of men about fatherhood." Fourteen men attended.

One of the most revealing features of these workshops has been that the men consistently expressed anxiety and concern that something was wrong with them or that they must be abnormal because they were feeling so confused about becoming or being new fathers. The men who attend these workshops really were desperate to hear how other new and expectant dads were doing. Most of the men shared in their concluding remarks that hearing the other fathers' stories about the difficulties and struggles they were having helped them realize that they were experiencing "what every new dad goes through."

The dads who have attended my workshops (or the ongoing fathers' groups I also offer now) often comment on how isolated they feel from other men/fathers. Most of the men in these workshops said they turn to their wives, not other men, to help them understand their feelings about fatherhood. With time I have come to understand that men/fathers share feelings quite easily when it is safe to do so, but what we as a community of men find especially lacking is the opportunity to have such meetings where the primary focus is on our feelings about being fathers.

Through the workshops and research I have conducted I have identified "Four Phases of Paternal Development." Each of these phases offers the man/father a unique opportunity to understand himself through his feelings rather than through his thinking about who he is. Often, when these two ways of "knowing" diverge, tension about our identity results. I see this as a healthy tension, one that is moving us towards a more integrated understanding of who we are as both thinking and feeling human being.

As men, we are taught to be cut off from our emotions early on in life. In fact if we do cry or show vulnerability we are told we are a "sissy" or are acting like a girl. Not only is this degrading toward women, but it characterizes feelings and emotions as something negative. It also unconsciously conditions us to equate feelings with women and the feminine, and teaches us that if we express how we feel (uncertain, scared, vulnerable, hurt, sad, frustrated, delighted, excited, inspired—to name a few feelings), we are acting like women or "girls" and are not masculine. This is where the conflicts and opportunities arise for men when they become fathers. In becoming a father we can, through the struggles of parenting, learn not just to nurture our children, but nurture the feeling part of ourselves that has been cut off by the cultural taboos of masculinity.

Over the years, the individual psychotherapy I have done with men leads me to believe that growing up in America can be an abusive experience for males. In part because of the lack of parental education and in part because of dramatic economic and social changes, children, but boys particularly, have been forced to be independent and self-sufficient much earlier than they are emotionally capable of. This forced premature "manhood" has created several generations of men who are either so "mature" that they seem rigid and controlling in their behavior, or else, at the other extreme, men who act like teenagers throughout their lives. Yet both these extremes of personality may be transformed by the man who, when he becomes a father, is willing to open himself up to the process and feelings in parenting and loving his children.

Much research has been conducted on women and motherhood whereas until recently, little work has been done on men and fatherhood. Historically, it has been assumed without much reflection that if a father was providing economically for the family, he was making his contribution. A successful economic provider was a "good father." Mothers were expected to provide the other essentials that their children needed. This had been the model for parenthood over the last hundred years: fathers provided the money, and mothers took care of the rest of the family needs.

All this has changed today. When fathers are cut off from the emotional life of the family, and only support their families through work, everyone suffers. Research shows that the less that fathers are involved emotionally in the day-to-day lives of their families, the lower the self-esteem, sociability, and problem-solving capacities their children have.

Mothers also suffer by having to carry the entire burden of the psychological well-being of their children. Unfortunately, much of modern psychology supports this by focusing mainly on the mother's influence on the child's emotional development, and ignoring the father's contributions— even if it is obvious that his influence is most greatly felt by his absence.

Today, all this is changing. In most families (85%) both parents work. The need for fathers to be more involved in the day-to-day lives of their families is a necessity. Perhaps since the women's movement has helped create opportunities for women to lead more well-balanced lives it has forced men to be more engaged in family responsibilities. I am sure in part this is true, but the men/fathers I have interviewed all talk about how they don't want to be the sole economic provider for their families, but want to be able to participate in caring for their children too. Recent studies bear this out, as most men (78%) interviewed say they would gladly give up career advancement for more time with their children. Why are men changing in this way? How is this happening?

There are four emotional transitions that men pass through as fathers that mark their character and define who they are as men. (1) The first is the man's understanding and resolution of his relationship with his own father. (2) The next involves the way confusion and emotional uncertainty, usually at pregnancy or birth (or through adoption or becoming a stepparent) presents him with an opportunity to become either more flexible or more rigid as a man. (3) Third is the ability to be dependent and to allow others to be dependent on him. (4) The last is how he is able to form affiliations with other fathers and move from isolation into community.

All these transitions lead the man/father to a greater sense of purpose in his life—what I like to call a deepening of his soul. Fatherhood can humanize a man like no other experience I can think of. The most profound contribution we have to give as men can be manifested through our parenting of the next generation. Ultimately, when we reflect on who we are as men we must ask how we have affected the lives of others. I would like now to explore more fully each of the four stages mentioned above.

(1) Masculinity and fatherhood are socially constructed. As times change, our expectations and constructs for whom we are as men adapt to the social and cultural needs of our families. This social flexibility is a positive quality for us as men. It liberates us from having to model ourselves after the past, and gives us the freedom to create what is most relevant for us and for our families today. This is not easy work. Many dads fear that because their own father was not a "role model" for them they don't know how to be a parent. The relationship a man has with his own father is one of the underlying themes he needs to resolve to become, not only the father he wants to be, but also the man he wants to be. Our own independent psychological life is not easy to achieve. The influence of our mothers and fathers runs deep. As men become fathers, their relationship with their own fathers seems to intensify. The working-through of the issues between father and son continues even after the father's death.

Recently, my psychotherapy practice I was consulting with a father whose own father had committed suicide. He came into therapy because his wife had been concerned about his seeming lack of interest in their young son. At first he complained about how much work demanded of him and how he was just tired, not uninterested in his son. He also remarked that when his son became more complex and "interesting," maybe around five, he was sure he would have a closer relationship with him then. All of these insights seemed reasonable. When I asked him about his own father, he had a very strong reaction.

His father had been quite involved with him as a baby and a young child. He had very positive memories of his father and of the pride his father felt for him. His attachment with his father was quite strong. He said his father's suicide took him by complete surprise and he was depressed for a couple of years after his death.

The more we talked about his father, the more the loss of this close, important relationship seemed to dominate his life. He had found it difficult after his father's death to develop close relationships. Not until he met his wife and experienced her steadfast commitment to him could he trust that people could be depended on. He began to recognize that the loss he felt from his father's unexpected suicide had undermined his confidence and trust in people. If he couldn't count on his father, whom could he trust? And as the therapy progressed he recognized with sadness and tears that he was keeping a distance from his own son to protect him. He was trying to protect his son from what had hurt him the most—the loss of his father. He realized that if his son was not close or attached to him, he would not suffer the pain of losing someone so dear, so important.

When he could understand that he was projecting his pain and loss onto his relationship with his son, another wave of sadness came over him. He realized how much his son needed him. He became aware of how he was holding himself back from giving his son what he needed, his alive and interested father. He said it was as if he was treating his son as though he had already died! The therapy continued, and as he experienced the depth and grief of his feelings for his own father, he became able to enjoy and parent his own son. He began to separate out his feelings of himself as a father from his feelings about his relationship with his own father. Although this may be a dramatic example, the pattern is clear with every man I have spoken with over the years. When they became fathers, the need to understand the relationship with their own dad was a psychological step that led to their own autonomy.

(2) The second transition that occurs through parenthood and adds dimension to men's character happens when they confront the change and

disorganization a child brings into their life. As I mentioned earlier, it is believed that to be masculine means to be in control. We have been socialized as boys to feel that control of our emotions is what makes us strong and desirable. In order to maintain that sense of control we need to cut ourselves off from about half of our emotional life—the fears and worries we all encounter.

Childbirth and parenting brings with it such uncertainty. It has often been referred to as the "crisis" stage in the couple's relationship. I think this term "crisis" misrepresents what is really happening. The connotation of "crisis" is that something has occurred that shouldn't have, and now we need to make things normal again by returning to the situation before the crisis. In my research I called this transition to parenthood phase for men the "emergent" phase. It seems that rather than a "crisis" occurring, a new definition of the man as a father is "emerging." He cannot go back to the way he was before, and must attain new potential in himself as a father. This new potential asks him to give up a degree of self-centeredness.

Before they have children, both men and women often don't realize how much flexibility and free time they have. After the baby is born, free time is so severely reduced that it is probably the most difficult transition the couple has to make—understanding that their life now involves a third person, who, particularly in the early years, needs one-on-one care. Responding to this transition can humanize us.

Being independent, focusing on one's own needs, not being "committed," is often depicted in the media as a romantic and attractive lifestyle. Hollywood worships the "eternal adolescent." The man who becomes a parent is usually dealt with in a comic fashion. We don't have a positive and life-affirming image as men as young or new fathers. We don't see fatherhood being pursued as a life choice for men. Finding value, fulfillment and creativity in parenthood is not an image Hollywood has found a way to cash in.

The confusion and uncertainty brought about by birth and the early years of parenting ask a man whether he can value and love others outside of himself. It challenges a man to feel himself as part of a group, his family, whose survival and emotional well-being he is part of.

I remember a young father I was seeing as he and his wife were preparing to become parents. He was certain that having a baby would not slow his life down. He was planning on taking up windsailing soon after the baby was born. He had also planned a trip to Mexico for them when the baby would be about 6 weeks old. He was unable to see that having a baby would change his routines, and that by creating and planning for the trip he was reassuring himself that he needn't look at the confusion and uncertainty he was feeling.

After returning from a very difficult trip to Mexico, getting little sleep, and unable to do the things he used to do while on vacation with his wife, he was wondering what had happened to their life. In the weeks that followed he was able to admit that not only wasn't he prepared for parenthood, he had no idea what to expect.

Out of the confusion and uncertainty which this young father fought hard against, he regained a sense of working in the present, and grew more focused on his current experience, and what it meant to him now. Maybe it was a necessity of survival, but his personality was shifting. At the end of therapy he was a less driven person; he seemed more at peace with the disorganization at hand. He commented on how much closer he felt to his wife and child. He still had plans and adventures for the future, but they did not take him away from the present. In our final sessions he talked a lot about how becoming a father had centered him in his life and in day-to-day experience. He was much less concerned with proving to others what an exciting and interesting person he was. He seemed more open to change and more aware of the value of his everyday experiences with his wife and child.

(3) The third transition a man undertakes when he becomes a father is allowing himself to be dependent on others. As John Wayne personified the man who could do it all for himself, today's dads must be able to need and value the need for others to depend on and to be depended on.

It is becoming clear to couples today that economic survival is interdependent. Both husbands and wives need to work. There is more gender equality in the workplace and home. Men have begun to appreciate that today it takes two parents working together, depending on each other—often just to get by financially. But more than financial dependency, it is emotional dependency that is changing men.

As men we have been raised to believe that if we need to depend on someone we are weak, helpless, and, worst of all, powerless. The old joke about "no matter how lost a man may get he'll never ask his wife for directions" illustrates this idea!

When men feel the vulnerability of their own children it can lead them to an appreciation for how much the members of a family need each other and how much they need to depend on others to feel whole. The opposite can also happen. Fear of the vulnerability and defenselessness a man encounters in his own child can cause him to shut down, to become removed. It is a powerful experience to realize we were all once at the mercy and good wishes of adults to guide us and nurture us till we could care for ourselves. If we as men were never able to feel we could depend on others, then having others depend on us seems almost intolerable.

In a special case I consulted on, this dependency became alarmingly clear. This man had a three-year-old son and came into therapy with his wife because they were having difficulty with their sex life. They were not having sex very often and he was both angry (which he expressed quite well) and hurt (which he hid very well). He demanded that his wife agree to have sex at least twice a week or he would either leave her or start having affairs. This was a tense and frustrated couple both sexually and emotionally. She felt also that she wanted to have sex more but often felt exhausted and more of the housemaid than his wife. As we talked it became apparent that in a marriage that is monogamous he was dependent upon his wife for sex. No matter what threats he made, no matter what other plans he might act on, if he wanted to remain monogamous (and in this case married) he needed to see that he needed and depended on his wife sexually. He struggled with the idea that he would have to depend on another to get his needs met.

We explored this theme of needing to depend on another to get his needs met. It took us back to his childhood when he was the good little boy who didn't need anyone. He remembered how his parents used to comment on how he was so mature that he hardly needed them. He began to understand how difficult it was for him to "ask" and not "demand" when he needed something. In fact, the couple had never had a dialogue about their sex needs in the relationship. It had been an argument about who was not being responsive to whom.

Over time he worked, as did his wife, through the dependency needs they had with each other. He began to feel more permissive with his son.

He felt more comfortable with his son's fears and immature behavior. At one point in the therapy he commented on how he was going to give his son time to grow up and not be rushed as he was.

(4) The fourth transition from man to father is the most difficult, but perhaps the most rewarding. It is also a transition that can make the other three transitions much easier. Understanding our relationship with our fathers; moving through the uncertainty that parenthood presents; understanding our dependency needs—all are phases leading us to be more emotionally caring, kind, and empathetic men. When we can share this journey of adult development with other dads we can learn from each other's experiences. I believe it is the isolation that we as men grow up with, the real lack of contact with other men, that makes our emotional lives so difficult to develop. We have to figure out so much on our own. It is hard to imagine that when we become fathers—the most important transition in our lives—we are often without other men to share and learn with.

This fourth phase is the affiliation and community phase where we must find a way to connect with a greater community. Part of this happens naturally when our kids enter kindergarten or first grade. We naturally meet other men. But in the early years of parenting, when it is most essential to have the support of other fathers, we are often alone.

In the fathers' groups and workshops I have conducted the old adage that men don't express their feelings just doesn't hold true. The fathers in my groups are overflowing with emotion on all the "transitions" I have just written about. What is missing for these men is not that they have difficulty expressing their feelings, but that they have few or no opportunities to do it. In a safe environment free from competition and one-upmanship, focusing on the importance of parenting, rich and important stories are told. Fears about the instability of marriage, angry, sad and abusive stories of our own fathers, stillbirths and abortions, work and family issues, dealing with in-laws, finding time for ourselves and our wives, concerns for schools and the environment, the meaning of sex in our lives— all are topics which father-to-father we discuss, argue, cry, and laugh about together. The men who come to these groups have to go to some trouble to be involved. It is not easy, readjusting schedules and having the willingness to make a commitment to a group of men. Concerns about how to have a close relationship with other men are often difficult to understand. What comes out of this experience with other fathers? The men have commented that talking about fatherhood with other dads has certainly given them more confidence in parenting. They also are clear that they understand much more about who they are as men. When I ask them how fatherhood has changed them as men, the response has been they feel that they are more sensitive, compassionate, tender, warm and understanding.

Our children, our wives, our society will all benefit from such a wonderful group of truly good men, that our children (and us, dad-to-dad) have helped us become.

For further self-reflection and discussion:

1. How has fatherhood changed you as a man?

2. What has been most rewarding about being a dad, and what have you worried about most?

3. What phase of fatherhood are you in now?

Nirvana is the Present Moment

right here
and now
it is happening
robin hopping
on the patio table
rosebush in full bloom
sea salt air from the Bay--
if you expect Nirvana, when you die
  whoops!
    you just missed it...

The Rites of Spring:
Hardball, Softball and Gender

In bringing up children, spend on them half as much money and twice as much time.
—*Author Unknown*

For the last six years I have been involved in coaching boys' Little League and girls' softball. Everything starts in January, when I fill out the application and make sure it gets mailed on time. Then I look at the team schedule for the season and figure out how I will adjust my schedule for the ten to twelve weeks of the season. Being a psychotherapist, I work two evenings a week. When the baseball season starts, I have to modify my evening schedule in order to be able to go to practice and then return to work for a couple of late-evening sessions. Perhaps if I were richer or more financially successful, I would not have to work those evenings. Unfortunately, as a result of the difference between the cost of living in the San Francisco Bay area and my wife's and my wages, I can't afford to lose the income from working those evenings. As in the stories I hear from so many fathers, we all learn to stretch ourselves to try and meet both the emotional and financial needs of our families.

Coaching baseball and softball is my most enjoyable "stretch." I am not a particularly avid fan of professional baseball, but the excitement of watching my children and their friends reminds me of all that is good and noble and engrossing about our national pastime. Both boys and girls bring to the game an energy and intensity that is very captivating and inspiring, and that their professional counterparts seem to lack. The lessons of life—working as a team, trying your best, learning how to lose, improving from your mistakes, enjoying personal success and sharing the pride of winning with friends—are all values that children's sports can bring us in contact with. The openness and naiveté that each child brings to the game challenges me as a coach to respond with equal sensitivity to his or her honest emotions.

Observing the difference between girls' softball and boys' hardball allows me to see how gender differences are tied to the social conditioning that we are subject to. Also, it is sad to see how boys are pushed to compete and win in order to prove their competence. I was not surprised to see that over 90% of the boys don't continue in organized sports after finishing Little League. I can remember when I played Little League thirty-five years ago. My coach interrogated me after I struck out because, he said, I did not show enough anger. I said I had tried my best, to which he responded that if I didn't get more upset after I struck out, he would take me out of the starting lineup. The next time I struck out I threw the bat against the bat rack, and the coach consoled me for my good try! I had obviously impressed him with my fake display of anger. It seemed as though this incident had convinced him that I had an intensity for the game.

As I began my Little League coaching career in AAA ball, the beginners' level, I went to view an upper-division game to see how it was coached. I was astonished to hear how the coach talked to the boys. Now, being a psychotherapist has its drawbacks, and perhaps having a natural interest in children's development makes me a bit more sensitive to how people communicate. But the criticism that was being leveled at the boys seemed extreme. When we began our season, I noticed distinct differences between coaching styles. Some of the men were without a doubt interested in supporting the boys at whatever level they could play, but others thought that winning was what it was all about. I was sure that I would be in the former group.

After our team lost its first four games, however, I found myself getting frustrated and wanting for my team to be "winners." It became easier to be disappointed in the boys when they missed a grounder, and harder and harder not to be discouraged after a poorly played inning. I found myself getting annoyed if the boys didn't play their hardest in each inning. I started to wonder what had happened to my own sensitivity and compassion. Where had I lost the conviction that it was just a game, and how had it become a contest? It was easy to get caught up in what I have always been trained to do, namely to be a "winner." The only problem is that the final score never really tells you who won the game. It took me years to learn this about life. I knew that I would like to be able to teach this to the children. Slowly, the art of coaching evolves, usually with the teamwork of the coaching staff. In Little League, it took working together and positive reinforcements from each coach on our team to preserve the fun in the game.

I was surprised to see how critical the boys were of each other. A strike or a missed grounder was often met with laughter or a put-down. It took some time for the boys to learn to comfort each other. This was sad for me to see. When the boys were assured that they could comfort a friend who cried when he struck out, the feeling of being a team began to develop. Our society asks boys to be very independent and very competitive early in their lives. I think this makes it harder for them to be supportive of each other. To express their benevolent feelings for each other means showing tenderness and emotion. Boys are told that to be independent, they must give up this tender side of their characters. Being good means achieving "mastery" for boys—and this relates to being in control of their emotions. I think I was a good coach for the Little League because I took a positive stand and said that it was okay to cry and to be upset and to have your friends reassure you. Mind you, not all the coaches supported my position that winning wasn't what it was all about, but it certainly helped with my group's team spirit.

In my experience, girls' softball is a completely different story! Being involved with my daughter's softball teams during the last few years has been a real eye-opener, showing me how positive sports can be. The league is organized around the idea that the game is fun. The coaches work cooperatively, and men and women coach together. The spirit of the girls as a team is present from the first day. The girls I have coached are in the second, third and fourth grades. I think two experiences I have had in coaching these girls sum up the differences between coaching the girls and coaching the boys.

First, I discovered that the girls do not want to get their friends "out" on the other teams. Last year, we had to spend the better part of one practice—an hour and a half—talking about how it feels to "make an out" on a friend. I also found that if a girl gets hurt on the field, all the other girls run to her and try to help. We had to ask that just the two or three girls closest to her help out, to keep some order during the game. The sentiment of concern for teammates runs high. The social spirit of the game is intense and the competitiveness I have seen seems to stem more from good fun and "sport" than from the values of winning or losing. The sense of mastery through winning does not appear to be a strong motivation in girl's softball.

I know that I have oversimplified much of what goes on in Little League and girls' softball. The point could be made that boys might gain from being less competitive and more team-oriented, and that girls could use a little more stimulation in the competitive realm. Of course, any of you who have coached know that coaching a team involves not only working with the children but working with the parents as well. The parents usually present the greater challenges. Coaching has challenged me to look at my own values about competition and winning. Sharing the experience with my kids has helped us all learn and struggle with what it means to be a team—which, come to think of it, is not so different from what it means to be a family!

For further self-reflection and discussion:

1. How does competition affect boys' relationship to each other?

2. How do we create equal opportunity for our daughters to be physical, assertive and competitive?

3. What are your feelings about the importance of being part of a team? Do you feel that exercise and staying in shape are important?

The Window

I was getting ready to go to work
to give a lecture.
I am putting my notes
in my briefcase
when the ball comes through the window,
the glass flying,
a million tiny knives all over the living room.
In that moment, I feel my anger begin to grow:
my frustration at this house,
never being organized enough,
the expense of getting the window fixed,
the temporary solution of living with cardboard
or an old piece of plywood,
thoughts of how will we
clean up all this glass--
my anger grows as I know I will be late
for my presentation.

I hear your small 4 ½ year old feet
running up the steps,
I see your small arm push
open the door,
your eyes look up to mine
moist, searching.

I take you in my arms:
"Are you hurt?"
It's o.k.,
it's only a window,
it can be replaced.
What's important is that you are not hurt,
it's only glass,
you are my son, I love you.
Let's get the broom."

Raising Sons

We've begun to raise daughters more like sons... but few have the courage to raise our sons more like our daughters. —Gloria Steinem

These were my thoughts when our son Morgan turned nine. Since his birth I have actively participated in his care. This has not always been easy. I think my first lesson was that men as fathers are expected to help their wives but not be too interested in actually caring for their children. Fathers should be helpful around the house but not wander too far into "women's territory."

When Morgan was a baby, I worked only part time so that I could share equally in his care. We made daily journeys to the park. We played in the sand with his trucks and talked with the moms who were there. Because I was the only man at the park with my kid, the consensus or assumption was that I was taking care of my child because I was unemployed.

I remember talking with a grandmother who was at the park. I told her that my wife and I both worked part time, that we didn't need to hire childcare and that I felt fortunate to be able to spend this time with my son, especially while he was a baby. She listened attentively. As I left the park she told me how much she had enjoyed talking with me, and said she hoped I would be able to get some work soon!

I lost count of the number of times women said how nice it was to see a man "mothering." I usually responded that they were actually observing fathering. I was not attempting to be a role model or make a political statement about men as fathers. I was taking action on what was important and meaningful to me.

So this was my first lesson. Procreation was part of being a man. Feeling one's potency through conception, this was definitely masculine. Yet wanting to care for a baby—no, this was not what being a man was about. At least that was the message I was getting. But that was just the beginning.

These early years with my son were wonderful and exciting—and like living with a Zen master. Morgan, like all young children, lived totally in the present. With him I learned about plants, bugs, flowers, cracks in the cement, and all the little details of life and our environment that usually passed me by.

It was when Morgan entered school that I got my real insight into what it means to grow up male in America. Just go to any elementary school and it is easy to ascertain how different boys and girls are. It also became evident that active and energetic boys are sometimes troubling for teachers. They can't sit still. Their curiosity is insatiable, and most elementary teachers (who are usually women) may not be tolerant of their exuberance.

Morgan had studied Martin Luther King and the Civil Rights Movement in the second grade. On our way home from school one day, Morgan told me that in his class the boys were being treated like the blacks in the South whom Martin Luther King was trying to help. I asked him what he meant. He said that if the girls talked out of turn or didn't listen, the teacher would ask them to please be quiet. If the boys did the same thing, she would yell at them and be very angry about how bad they were.

Shaming starts early. To be a man in America means to grow up with a large dose of shame—shame about your energy, and desire and shame about your body. Morgan's experiences began to remind me of what I had heard so often in school as a child: "You're too excited and you can't sit still. What's wrong with you that you can't sit still?" Why was it wrong to be excited? Why was it bad to feel this way? What a terrible body I must have, that I couldn't sit without moving. If the words themselves weren't shaming, the tone was.

Morgan has learned many wonderful things in school, and he has developed and worked out many important relationships. He has had great, mediocre and bad teachers. My wife and I have tried to guide him to situations that were socially and academically life-enhancing. I would be in denial not to say that boys are treated very differently in school than girls are. At least at the elementary level. And so much of our creativity and feeling is shamed out of us. The exuberance of a third- or fourth-grade boy is a dangerous experience.

The next insight on what it means to be a man has to do with competition. I am amazed and appalled by the level of competitiveness I see among young boys. It begins with athletics and then permeates all other aspects of their lives. What I see is that by the fourth grade a pecking order—a hierarchy—is already established. That hierarchy seems to grant each child a limited potential of feelings and expression. It is the beginning of our life-long experience with isolation from our peers. In my son's case, I see the absence of adult males in any area other than athletics. There are so few men in the schools to model other ways of being and feeling.

The competitiveness goes far beyond athletics. Who has the best new toy? Whether it concerns a new book or a new Nintendo game, there is a real lack of appreciation for the other boy's experience. It becomes threatening to these eight- and nine-year-olds if a friend has something of value.

How well that translates to my experience as an adult male and the difficulty I see in myself, sometimes, in being able to support and appreciate the achievements of other men! I understand this intellectually, but on the level of feeling it goes deep. Watching my son's experience with his friends, it is obvious how I acquired these feelings.

At Morgan's ninth birthday party he had ten of his friends sleep over. In the morning, the "gang," as we called ourselves, walked to the bakery. On the way home, one of the boys tripped on the sidewalk and fell. He was crying. Immediately everyone laughed and made fun of him. They had learned it is shameful to cry and were shaming their friend with laughter. I held the hurt boy. I called all the other boys around me. I told them that the men I know would help out a friend if he was hurt. I said "real" men would show their strength by caring about what happened to a friend.

I was not prepared for their response. They began to ask their crying friend where his hurt was. They crowded around and put their arms around him. As we continued to walk home, each boy talked with him individually about his tripping on the sidewalk. The whole interaction shifted, and I don't think it was due to the "eloquence" of what I had said.

It became apparent that these boys had absorbed what I said as if it were water and they were walking through a desert. They thirsted for some validation from an adult male who would say that it is alright to have concerned feelings for a hurt friend. It's OK to cry. I am sure they all knew the loneliness of being teased when they got hurt. I just told them that men care about their friends and show concern about what happens to them. A simple message.

Where are the men—fathers, brothers, uncles, cousins, neighbors, mentors, political leaders and teachers—to carry this simple message to our children?

The shaming, the competitiveness we experience as children, cuts us off from appreciating ourselves and others. My son has, through his journey, reminded me of how painful a process it is for boys to grow up in America. I hope that by participating in his life I have helped him to develop some skillful means for finding antidotes to shaming and competitiveness. By being present in his life, and with the help of my male friends, I hope he will see a wide range and depth of feeling experienced and expressed by different men.

Perhaps growing up male in America is basically an abusive experience. We as men can help each other recover from our shame and competitive/ isolating lives. (Much has been said about this in the recent men's movement.) Let us begin our own healing by respecting and nurturing the sons, daughters and children that we know.   ▲▲

For further self-reflection and discussion:

1. What feelings do you have about this essay?

2. Do you remember any similar situations from your childhood?

3. Can men be strong, tender and masculine at the same?

Sweet Sadness

Morgan and I are getting out of the car to visit the
junior high school he will be attending this fall.
His hair is sticking up in the back and he asks me
to straighten it. He is an eleven year old boy and
how his hair looks has become very important.
I have a pocket comb in my briefcase. I take it out
and straighten his "part" and comb down the back
of his hair. I know this may be one of the last times
he will ask for my help in this way. I watch as each
hair passes through the comb and comes to rest
against his head as if it were a silken feather.
And he is now a young strong hawk, beginning to
soar away from his nest. He will not want to be
helped much more like this. I take pride in his
independence and spirit. And I grieve in silence for
this time, when he needs me to comb his hair.

—Bruce Linton (journal notes 1992)

A New Interpretation of an Old Myth: Oedipus Rex Reconsidered

I cannot think of any need in childhood as strong as the need for a father's protection.
—*Sigmund Freud*

Sigmund Freud was a physician whose interest in neurology led to the development of modern psychology. He used the Oedipus story from Greek mythology to express how strongly young boys may be attached to their mothers' love. He felt that this story explained what he considered to be an unconscious process in which a young boy rejects his father so that he can have his mother's love all to himself. The Oedipal complex and the Oedipal phase of development have become commonplace in the terminology of childhood psychology. Working through the Oedipal phase, young boys separate from their mothers and begin to develop their sense of themselves as men. Unfortunately, if one accepts the traditional interpretation of Freud, it means that boys must reject their mothers (and the femininity that their mothers represent) in order to develop their own identity and masculinity. This not only devalues mothers and women, but cuts off boys' connections to the feminine principle, which limits their development of a more whole and well-rounded psychological/emotional life.

Let's reconsider the Oedipal myth. The story of Oedipus begins with King Laius and Queen Jocasta of Thebes. Laius learns of a prophecy from the oracle of Delphi that he and his wife will have a son who will kill his father and marry his mother. When their son is born, Laius has the newborn child left on a hillside to die so that the prophecy cannot be fulfilled.

The infant boy, Oedipus, is found by a shepherd and raised by King Polybus of Corinth. Oedipus hears the prophecy as a man and leaves Delphi and Corinth, fearing that he will kill Polybus, who he believes to be his real father. On his journey Oedipus encounters an arrogant, rich nobleman who orders him off the road. Oedipus kills the man, who turns out to be Laius, in a duel. Oedipus ends up outside the city of Thebes, which is terrorized by a Sphinx and can only be saved by someone who can answer the Sphinx's riddle. Oedipus answers the riddle, the Sphinx kills herself, and

Oedipus is honored by the whole city. Queen Jocasta has lost her husband and Oedipus is deemed a good match for her, so they marry, fulfilling the prophecy. When Oedipus becomes aware that the prophecy has come true, he blames himself for all that has happened, and blinds himself.

In my interpretation, this myth says more about fathers than it does about boys. It is the father who is jealous and fearful that his son will marry his wife and become king. The father is worried that his son will replace him, and this is what motivates him to attempt to kill his own child. It seems more like a father–son complex to me than a mother–son problem. Why doesn't the father protest the prophecy? Why does Freud choose to ignore the father's conscious and cruel behavior toward his son?

In working as a psychotherapist with couples who have young children, I find that the Oedipal theme of paternal jealousy is common. Many men were the primary focus of their mate's attention prior to the birth of their child. New fathers often report feelings of jealousy because of all the attention the baby is getting and the neglect they feel as a result. New fathers often have a conscious wish to go back to the relationship they had before the baby was born. Helping couples develop into a family and adjust to being parents requires having fathers come to terms with these feelings of jealousy, abandonment and lack of attention from their mates.

I think it is time to re-examine the Oedipal myth in terms of what it is saying about a father's unconscious feelings regarding the early stages of parenthood. The fear of a son or daughter becoming the primary recipient of his mate's attention and affection, and the possibility that the child will replace him as the "king" within the family, are very difficult concepts for a new father.

In Freud's interpretation, fathers can displace their own emotional difficulties onto their children and then punish them for the normal loving relationship that exists between mothers and children. Projecting onto innocent children the feeling of wanting to murder their father for desiring their mother's love appears to me to reflect more on a father's fears and jealousies than anything else.

As fathers today, we need to recognize the mythology that has guided our development. As we create a new definition of fatherhood, we must examine the fears and educate ourselves about aggressive feelings that becoming parents stirs within us. We must come to terms with our own emotional projections and breathe new meaning into a mythology that honors our children and mates. It may not be an easy task to reflect on our own emotional vulnerabilities, but it is one we can help each other with as we grow and develop in our relationships and lives.

For further self-reflection and discussion:

1. Are you jealous of the relationship between your partner and your baby? If so, how does the jealousy manifest itself?

2. How do you handle the frustration when your child's needs must come before your needs?

3. When you were growing up, how did your mother and father reconcile their needs as individuals and as a couple with your needs as a child?

Father

I waited for the sound of your truck to drive down
the block,
waiting for you to come.
I waited, baseball glove and bat
in hand.
I waited on our front lawn for
you to play catch with me, maybe
help me with my batting.

I learned to recognize the sound of your old Ford
truck
from three blocks away.
I could close my eyes and listen for you.
I would open my eyes just as you pulled in the
driveway.

I got home at 3 and you at 6
and I would wait for you,
throwing the ball up into the air,
catching it myself.
I waited for you.

Mom knew where she could find me
waiting out in front for you.

You would arrive, get out of your truck smelling like
chickens,
give me a big hug and tell me you were too tired to
play.
I would stay out on the lawn
holding my glove, bat and ball,
wondering what was wrong with me.

How Dads Influence Psychological Development

Nothing has a stronger influence psychologically on their environment and especially on their children than the unlived life of the parent. —Carl Jung

Through infancy, childhood and adolescence we are dependent on our parents to help us gradually learn how to cope with the world around us. They are there to admire us, stimulate us, protect us and teach us in ways that are attuned to our tendencies and help our creative talents emerge. I believe it is the primary task of parenting to teach children the skills for living that allow each child to deal with the difficulties and disappointments in life without being overwhelmed. I am going to discuss how fathers participate in some unique ways in facilitating this learning.

In terms of interpersonal relationships, the father facilitates the young boy's social learning about communicating and relating to others. Boys with fathers who can be emotionally present and warm acquire interpersonal skills that allow them to find satisfaction in developing attachments with others. The father is indispensable in helping his son with the integration of his aggressive feelings and the activation of what Jungians call the heroic process.

When dads are not emotionally present for boys, especially at adolescence, they have no one to form a positive same-sex identification with, and either cannot separate from their mother, or must devalue her. Often in devaluing their mother to define their own sense of maleness, they must alienate all that is feminine within them. The father is instructive in helping boys find satisfaction in their creative efforts and assists them in developing a sense of intimacy through both achievement and participation with others. Without this guidance and instruction often the only intimate feelings men develop is through their sexuality. The hormonal changes at adolescence provide a new challenge to the developing self. Having a father who can help a boy find satisfaction in his creative achievements can enable the son to see his libidinal energy manifest in ways other than sexual.

For girls, the first male relationship in their life is their father. He helps facilitate their self-esteem through active support of their interests. Since it is well accepted in our culture that men and males are the "special," privileged ones, what fathers take interest in is automatically of value. A father choosing to participate in the events in his daughter's life confirms that she is a priority for him and thus something of value. Fathers offer their daughters an alternative to the identity of woman = mother. A father's emotional support validates and confirms the daughter's ability to negotiate in the world. If a father is aware of the erotic feelings stimulated in him by his daughter and doesn't act them out, he confirms her plurality of being: she can be other than a mother. He facilitates her exploration of other dimensions of her personhood. Critical is the father's respect for the necessary privacy and modesty in order to allow his daughter's developing self to emerge. A father's role in menses is important to mention. This initiation into womanhood is the mother's ritual but the father must be able to mirror positively this transition in support of his daughter's developing sexuality.

Within the construct of the developing sense of work and career and its place in one's life, the father's support and interest are important. His own attitude toward his achievement seems to be the key factor. A father must continue to develop his own talents and interest to find satisfaction in his own life. This is the only way to communicate this potential to his children.

There are many negative stereotypes fathers have to overcome. Fatherhood appears to be a social construct adapting and changing to the social and economic conditions of the times. It becomes the responsibility of men as a community to address the needs, desires and aspirations that fatherhood entails for us. Men and fathers today are sincere and courageous in their consciousness-raising and self-reflection in asking themselves: In what ways do we contribute meaningfully to the societies to which we belong?

Not that long ago, there was a strong cultural belief in God and a political hierarchy of kings. We have lost those structures as social supports—in many cases for the better. We now live in a more equitable democratic world. But with the loss of God and king, these layers of "father projection" have fallen on the ordinary everyday dad. How does the everyday father inspire and guide his children in these morally challenging times?

Margaret Mead said, "Men are a biological necessity but a social inconvenience." How do we move as men into elevating the status of parenting, when the unconscious sentiment devalues our ability to nurture?

To address the question of the father transference in individual psychotherapy, let me say that images of the father are projected onto the therapist in the transference relationship. Transference occurs when a person takes the perceptions and expectations of one person, such as their father or mother and identities them onto another person. They then interact with the other person as if that person is the pattern they have transferred to them. At first the real sex or age of the therapist may play a part in facilitating or hindering the emergence of this material. There are many ways in which paternal imagery can enter into the therapy. The therapist may experience the transference as he/she becomes the positive father to replace the real-world negative father. He/she may become the "transferred" father to compensate for the "missing" external father. If the client had a very negative emotional experience of fathering there is a good chance the therapist will become the recipient of the projected transference of the bad father. He/she may also receive the transference for the idealized father, perhaps in hopes of mediating an earlier more negative experience of fathering. Hopefully, as therapists become more sensitive to the importance of paternal imagery their own work can incorporate this new material.

The case vignettes that I am going to present today reflect some of the important themes I see in relation to the father's impact on individual development. I will highlight the areas of interpersonal relationship, gender identity, and career choices.

I believe that the psychotherapy experience offers a "do-over." A "do-over" is what in my childhood we used to call a play in baseball, kickball or football, where we couldn't decide on the fair outcome of the play, so we would agree to do the play over. In psychotherapy, clients have the opportunity to return to the feeling-states where the essential process of their self was frustrated or where developmental arrests occurred. The needs and vulnerabilities that were developmentally impaired, in the essential early experiences, can be re-experienced within therapy with different outcomes. New internal psychological structure can form. And if the psychotherapist is good enough a new paradigm of development can begin. (It's never too late to have a happy childhood!)

I think it is important to note that most of the clients presented in these cases did not come in seeking psychodynamic therapy. Most came with specific problems relating to family and interpersonal issues and often were very unsophisticated about psychotherapy. With many of the people I work with, this is where we start; hopefully we end with a successful resolution to a troubling problem. Others decide to stay and work further on themselves, and in the process become educated about the therapeutic relationship itself. In this way we move into deeper issues. In my practice, my first goal is to be clinically useful to the client. Being a good listener and developing empathetic attunement to my clients is what I have found to be of greatest value. Of course, I always hope to be able to give the profound interpretation at the ripe moment…but I hope to spare my clients from too many mistakes and misunderstandings on my part, and err instead on the side of being the "good enough" therapist.

These cases focus on what I would consider to be "father material." Of course, there are many more aspects to analyze and explore, but it is my hope that these vignettes prove illustrative of how the father may appear in the interpersonal interactions our clients present to us.

The first case I want to discuss is how a man's relationship with his own father can become reenacted with his own child. In my work with fathers, I have found that understanding the relationship with their own father is central to their experience of parenting. I will refer to my client as Bill in this case vignette. (The case of Bill of also appears in the chapter "From Man to Dad" on page 42. This chapter is a professional paper I have modified for this book.)

Bill came into therapy because his wife had been concerned that he seemed uninterested in their young son. At first, Bill complained about how much work demanded from him and how he was just tired, not uninterested in being with his son. He also commented that when his son grew a little older, maybe around five, he was sure he would have a closer relationship with him. All of these observations seemed reasonable. When I asked Bill about his own father, he reacted very strongly. He said that his father had been quite involved with him as a baby and as a young child. He had very positive memories of playing with his father and of the pride that his father felt for him. His attachment to his father was quite strong. He said that his father's suicide took him by complete surprise and that he was very depressed for several years after his father's death. Bill was in his late teens when his father died. The more we talked about his father, the more it seemed that the loss of this close, important relationship seemed to dominate his life. He had found it difficult after his father's death to develop close relationships. Not until he met his wife and experienced her steadfast commitment to him could he trust and depend on another person. He began to recognize that the loss of his father had undermined his confidence and trust in people. If he couldn't count on his father, whom could he trust?

As the therapy progressed, he recognized with sadness and tears that he was keeping his distance from his own son to protect him. He was trying to protect his son from what had hurt him the most: the loss of his father. He realized that if his son was not close or attached to him, he would not suffer the pain of losing someone so dear, so important. When he could understand that he was projecting his pain and his loss onto his relationship with his son, another wave of sadness came over Bill. He realized how much his son needed him. He suddenly understood how much he had been depriving his child. He said it was as if he was treating his son as though he had already died! As the therapy continued, he began to separate out his feelings about being a father from his feelings about his relationship with his own father.

It is clear that men need to understand their relationships with their own fathers in order to understand themselves as fathers. In ancient times, fathers would acknowledge their sons' autonomy by giving them their blessing. Today, often in therapy, the father's blessing comes through the son's hard work at deciphering the unique relationship, for better or worse that he had with his own father. The freedom of emotion that comes when men understand the importance of their relationships with their fathers is critically linked to their enjoyment as parents.

Men as fathers will often either overcompensate for the lack of attention and emotion from their own fathers, or as in this case, try to shield their child from the loss or brutality/abuse they may have experienced with their own fathers by distancing or withdrawing from the relationship.

Also common to new fathers is the profound change in the relationship with their wives. In Bill's case, I was aware that the mother's primary maternal preoccupation (the child) caused him to feel again that he had lost someone dear to him. Her normal focus and preoccupation was on the baby, not on Bill. This may have reactivated his feelings of loss and caused him to view his child as the "reason" for his loss of his wife's attention. This could also be an unconscious motive for distancing himself from his child.

Bill came to consult with me because of my specialty in working with fathers. He felt some confidence in trying therapy with an "expert," who he hoped would understand his unique needs. It was up to me to be able to listen and support his insights about his fathering in a nonjudgmental way. This initial mirroring is essential for establishing a therapeutic alliance. In this case, it helped create the empathetic connection which allowed me to help Bill connect himself with his positive feelings about his intimate relationship with his father. The conflict between valuing the positive re-lationship Bill felt with his dad and his anger at the betrayal at his father's suicide induced the tension that he resolved by distancing from his own son. I was able to work with Bill's feelings of grief to move this case to a positive conclusion.

The second case I would like to present is one of a 55-year-old woman, whom I shall refer to as Jill. Jill was a social worker employed by a large social service agency, where she was having difficulties with her boss. Jill came to the first session and was so exceptionally nervous that she trembled and had a great deal of difficulty speaking. It appeared that although she felt unjustly criticized by her boss, she was not capable of complaining or commenting—in reality, not entitled to. Jill wanted immediate help and was frightened of losing her job.

Jill had a father who was critical of both her and her mother. The fam-ily rule was not to question the father. The father was the sole provider for the family, the mother was dependent on him and felt limited in her ability to stand up to him for herself or her daughter. Although she did well in school and was obviously a very intelligent woman, Jill was discouraged by her father from developing academically. The mother and father gave her the message that finding a man to take care of her was her destiny.

With regard to the circumstance of Jill's father, there are certain fac-tors that are important for our consideration. One is the convention of her time, which assumed that women were dependent on men. Therefore Jill's father may have been threatened by Jill's intelligence and potential beyond being a wife and mother. Jill did have a brother with whom the father bonded. The emotional distance between the mother and father may have led to family "taking sides," with the boys on one side and the girls on the other.

That Jill did not marry and have a family may have been all she could do to individuate herself from her mother, particularly because her father was not able to help her get beyond the assumption that "woman=mother." Jill was an attractive woman and her father may also have been threatened by her developing sexuality during adolescence. This might have led him to create increased distance from her.

Jill had never seen a male therapist, although she had been to therapy on and off for many years. I was very interested in hearing Jill's difficulties, something she had rarely experienced with a man. She often felt that she should be "taking care of me," and would often minimize her distress so as not to upset me. When I was able to interpret this, we could go more deeply into her feelings. (And I would often reassure her that I was here for her and that I was fine, and if I had any difficulties I could talk with my consultant or therapist.)

Central to Jill's case was the lack of entitlement. The "do-over" that transpired in the therapy that was most helpful for Jill was that I could support her in her professional development and she could allow a man to value her intellectual abilities. Together we worked on a letter which Jill sent to the program director, commenting on her difficulties with her boss. She asked to be transferred to another position. She was able to transfer to a job she felt much better suited for without any loss of pay. Jill was well received in her new position by her co-workers and found the job more satisfying. A few months later, her old boss was fired. As we worked on Jill's entitlement issues, we worked through not only her mother's passivity with Jill's father, but her own negative internalized father, which kept her from experiencing career satisfaction. Jill continued to find success at work and eventually sought and found a new job with another company that advanced her career, as well as her career satisfaction.

What was important about our work was that Jill could finally find the recognition, support and admiration for her intelligence and experience. Her positive transference onto me as a man/father substitute for a developmental loss allowed her to give herself, through psychotherapy, the internal positive nurturing father she missed in her family. The critical voice within lessened. The "do-over" of the therapy provided Jill the paternal acknowledgement she needed to reduce the normal tensions she experienced in the working world. She found she could make the professional transitions that would provide her with satisfaction.

This work may have been helped by my being a man. But I think any good psychotherapist who can attach to the paternal aspect that connects us to the world of work could provide the environment for an individual like Jill to discover and validate her professional competence.

The third vignette is one in which I started to see the couple together and then continued on to work with the husband. I shall refer to him as Rex. The couple had come to me to work out some of their early parenting issues, around areas like who gets up with the baby at night, and what is the equitable division of housework vs. earning money.

Both Rex and his partner had come to be parents in their early 40s. Although Rex was well educated and quite bright, he was marginal in his career and made barely enough money to contribute his half of the monthly expenses. When Rex began working with me alone, he complained about his wife's lack of sexual responsiveness. Having worked with them as a couple, I knew there were some valid concerns in this area. But Rex had received several complaints from women friends about his inappropriate hugs. He would squeeze them too tight and hold them too long. He had also flirted with the idea of having a homosexual affair with one friend who was willing, but finally hesitated about acting on it. On several occasions, Rex's wife asked him to talk to me about the comments he had made at a party or when they had friends for dinner. These comments were often charged with sexual material that others responded to negatively. Rex was always surprised by the negative response and talked about how he was the only spontaneous one in the group. He was a classic borderline personality with narcissistic tendencies.

In two years of individual therapy, we were able to make progress on both Rex's career underachievement and his need to sexualize much of his interaction with others. Both these issues were closely linked with his father. Rex's father, a writer, was, as Rex described him, often moody and withdrawn (depressed). As I have seen with many adult men, their career destiny seems to be closely linked to how they viewed their fathers at adolescence. Often fathers experience their mid-life transition as their children become adolescents. At midlife, the acceptance of things not done or goals not met can erode the father's sense of purpose. His son will pick up on his depression and often internalize this to interpret work as a burden, an overbearing responsibility—a type of indentured servitude. This is related, not so much to the father's achievement, as to his attitude toward achievement. His attitude toward achievement is manifested in his personality, and it is that attitude his children emulate.

To further complicate matters, I have observed that, in adolescence, particularly for boys, it is the father's "work" to help them direct their libidinal drive into areas of personal achievement and satisfaction. Writing, artistic exploration, music, poetry, athletics—whatever the endeavors be, these activities help them find a way of relating intimately in the world and finding gratification through achievement. Without this possibility, all that remains is for the sexuality to become the only environment for self-satisfaction.

Rex's parents had a bond that he often felt excluded from, and he also needed to compete with his two older brothers for his parents' attention. He saw his mother's attentiveness to his father mainly manifested in their sexuality. It appeared that the mother would help stimulate the father out of his depression by their sexual relationship. This relationship around sexuality is what Rex viewed as the "good stuff," and the only demonstration of his father's vitality.

As we proceeded in the therapy, Rex left many sessions discontent. He eventually organized his career and went on to become more at peace with the work world. He even enjoyed moderate success. He worked very diligently on his feelings about his sexuality and ultimately found satisfaction within his marriage. In one of our later sessions he confided in me that he started to work on paintings, and was keeping it secret. He joked that he may not be having as much sex as he would like, but his painting was becoming expansive—and it felt great.

For further self-reflection and discussion:

1. How have you internalized your father?

2. How has your parent's relationship influenced you?

3. What potential in you did your father or mother not understand about you?

You Are Not the Cause

You are not the cause of anyone's unhappiness
your own desires are important
you are not selfish for wanting what is most precious

we turn to each other with questioning eyes:
are you my mirror?
can you reflect what is most sacred in me?

why do we ask this, what is the need?
do we know who we are through the eyes of each
other?

What the Changing Roles for Women Means for Fathers

Parenting is hard. Balancing work and family is hard. Kids are kids. Our families are not accessories to our lives or objects we can control completely. And if we want to be the sort of parents to raise children of character and integrity, we have to unselfishly give a great deal of ourselves to the project. —Author Unknown

One of the lasting changes that came out of the 1960s was the Women's Movement. What women began as a revolution, however, has become an evolution. Both women and men are continuing to move away from traditionally defined gender roles. While these role changes have perhaps been more visible for women, men are moving at their own pace towards new possibilities. The changes in role expectations are opening up a new world for men who want to be fathers. The egalitarianism that is now possible among couples allows men to express their deep desire and ability to nurture and care that was previously the object of social disapproval.

Men are beginning to feel that they have a choice between spending time at work and taking time to be with their children while they grow up. Men who were able to take advantage of this possibility began to report a very deep feeling of satisfaction as well as personal growth, which they experienced by being with and caring for their babies. As other men viewed this new role-making behavior and began to hear men recount the peak experience of being present at their children's birth, the notion of becoming a father began to take on new meaning.

In the new potentials of being fathers, men see the possibility to express themselves through nurturing; there appears to be something very attractive about this for many men. Maybe this nurturing quality has been dormant within men for decades. Perhaps watching their children being born triggers some ancient biological process. As men spend more time with their children, new images of what it means to be a "real man" are being created.

What is going on in the men's movement? Do we really need a movement? Since most of the institutions in our society are designed and controlled by men, what do we really want to change?

War, incest, poverty, racism and the relationship between men and women are not separate and independent issues but interconnected and part of our social value system. Any men's movement that does exist owes a great debt to the women's movement and the development of feminist philosophy/ psychology in the United States. Since the 1960's women have been championing the causes of equality and equity both in the work world and in family life. Thus, for 50 years they have led the struggle to improve education and childcare.

Today's media-driven men's movement has ignored fatherhood. This has been my personal experience as I have participated in groups and workshops over the past twenty-five years, and it was one of the reasons for my starting the Father's Forum in 1986. In groups with Robert Bly and Michael Mead, and in my own men's groups and activities here in Northern California, I found a wonderful community of men. I discovered that the competitiveness and isolation I was taught to value was keeping me from being part of a community. The losses I carried within and never expressed were slowly eating me up from the inside. I began to understand how the unconscious devaluing of women had cut me off from a more nurturing part of myself. Through myth and stories, but mostly in the care of men— some older, some younger—I found a place to tell my stories. I became aware of how little opportunity I had had to talk about life, and the struggles of my own experiences, with other men. This is the greatest gift of the men's movement—to have the opportunity to safely talk with other men about the inner experiences of day-to-day living. This is the most healing and politically radical change the men's movement has created.

It was not until I had children myself that I began to realize that the issues of being a father and having a family were not being addressed by my "men's work." Talking about what it means to be a man is important, but if it does not connect us to the greater issues of our lives, then the men's movement is a failure. If the men's movement causes a greater schism between men and women than already exists, then it has failed doubly.

I think the most vital aspect of today's men's movement—and the least publicized and understood—is fatherhood. A fundamental shift is taking place in our society. We are aspiring to transition from a hierarchical to a partnership culture. Here we find that work and home life, making mon-

69

ey and raising children, are becoming cooperative ventures by men and women.

What today's fathers are doing all over the country is a grass-roots political movement. When men become fathers, an opportunity for a profound and fundamental emotional shift in consciousness arises. The vulnerability of their children can touch their own fears and vulnerabilities, and an emotional awakening can occur. This awakening is not just to the world of feelings. It is a connection to the world of greater political realities that they must now struggle with. It is the experience of "generativity" that carries the father from his own concerns about his identity as a man to the greater concerns for his family and community.

For years the men's movement has attempted to help men develop from the narcissistic stage of manhood to more dynamic involvement in our society. Today's fathers are fulfilling this aspiration. Our sense of manhood, what kind of person we want to be—beyond gender definition—is what today's dads struggle with. I see it over and over again in my fathers' groups. Men are reintegrating the nurturing and generative aspects of their emotional lives, and are coming to terms with a new definition of what it means to be a man, a definition which includes how to contribute to a society worthy of bringing children into.

Understanding what it takes to be a parent—the sleepless nights and endless patience, feeling the fears and vulnerabilities of having young children, worrying about education and childcare, figuring out how to provide guidance, setting limits without injuring your child's spirit, living equitably with your partner, being a parent and a husband, crafting a loving marriage and a family with values, morals and ethics—these are the challenges for today's dads. Sharing these struggles with other men/fathers helps create a community of men who are not only raising their consciousness about being men but about the society we live in.

It is my hope that as the respective men and women's movements continue to develop, we will see that our similarities outweigh our differences. We can live together as allies and raise children who will reflect all the best of what it means to be not just men or women, but truly caring human beings.

For further self-reflection and discussion:

1. Are men and women being socialized differently than in the past? How so?

2. What "feminine" qualities do you feel would help you as a man?

3. Are there subtle ways that you devalue women, or do you deal with the men and women in your life equally?

Depression

While looking at a picture of Pablo Neruda and
Matilde Urrutia
I am saddened by their happiness.
The strength of them holding each other reminds
me
of my emptiness with you.
A large boulder of depression rests over our love--
how long can this go on?
What do we do?
I have no answers.
Everyday my body feels numb.
I wake up to a dream,
walk around all day without a heart,
and wait for the night
to envelop me
into its blackness.

Divorce: Being the Best Dad You Can Be, No Matter the Circumstances

Our most basic instinct is not for survival but for family. Most of us would give our own life for the survival of a family member, yet we lead our daily life too often as if we take our family for granted. —Paul Pearshall

Divorce and parenthood are common occurrences in today's world. The current research on separation and divorce and its effects on children are not definitive. We do know that divisiveness and hostility between parents create emotional conflicts for children. And this is true whether the parents are married or divorced. But every family and every parent–child relationship is unique and has too many variable human factors to project the outcome of the child's self-esteem, personality, or success in life simply because their parents were divorced.

After the millennium, post-divorce fathering still needs to be better understood. There is still an unconscious prejudice about the father's interest and involvement with his children after divorce. It has been my experience from my clinical work that many fathers actually improve the quality, consistency, and interest in taking care of their children when faced with the realities of divorce. Divorce defines their time and involvement with their children in a way that the nuclear family may marginalize by having the mother is the presumed "default" that sees to it that their needs are met. It is often after divorce that dads know in detail about student–parent conferences, dates, and times of activities—and do take charge of those things for their children that they may have conveniently left for their wives to do when married.

The focus of this book has been how to recognize the important emotional challenges you face as a father. If you have recognized some of these challenges in earlier chapters, you probably have been conscious about your parenthood and its importance to both you and your children. Just keep up the good work! Trust that you have been an important part of your child's life and nothing can change that. But be aware of these dangers during the divorce process.

Voluntary custody agreements are often far better than court-ordered arrangements. It also shows your child that even with the difficulties that exist between you and your partner that when it comes to their best interest you can work together. Second, avoid the "Disneyland Dad" syndrome. This is where we as fathers feel guilty, or that we need to win our child's favor, so we overindulge them. If you have had a positive relationship with your child, trust in your connection and love and know that they will want to be with you. Of course, the age of your child at the time of your divorce will be important. The developmental needs of a six year old will be very different from those of a sixteen year old.

Divorce appears to be one of the most significant challenges fathers face. Just the thought of your child being in "custody" of one parent or the other has a bad feeling to it. Isn't "custody" what happens to suspected criminals? And the thought of asking permission from a former spouse to be with your child—not easy. The hurt and anger that may develop in divorce can contaminate your ongoing relationship with your child. Finding the best way to be with them may be hard, and the option of giving up and drifting apart often seems like the way to minimize the frustration and anger of a difficult divorce. If you have built an ongoing relationship with your child, then they know you are their father and an important person in their life. If you have not had as close a relationship as you may have wished, then a regular schedule after divorce may help you become a larger part of your child's life.

Finding satisfaction as a divorced dad takes work. Both your outer and inner worlds are changing. Refocusing your priorities between your work and parenting schedules; thinking about your life apart from marriage; integrating your friends, other potential mates, former in laws and grandparents—all these are challenges and relationships you need to reflect on. And we live in a culture that has rewarded men for economic and career success, not for emotional and nurturing behavior. All that needs to change in an obvious way when you are a divorced dad. Your nursing emotional side needs to rise to the demands of providing for your child in an obvious way. You will be on your own to comfort and calm your child both physically and emotionally when they are with you.

The idea that when we get divorced we are now "single" needs to change. We are never really single people; we are always part of a family.

It may be a family of biological relationships, or one of friends, but we are never just a person without a context. That is especially true when you are a father. But divorce often brings up many contradictory feelings as a result of the loss of the daily routines and the familiarities that give our life connections. But there can also be the relief of knowing that, for whatever reasons your relationship with your spouse could not continue, you can now use this profound life change as an opportunity for new possibilities for you and your child. The future may seem uncertain, but who is to say that this uncertainty is not actually filled with potential.

Five "strategies" for making the most of being a divorced dad:

1. Divorce happens—your fault, her fault, or no one's fault…life is filled with change. Uncertainty is frightening. Care about yourself, admit the loss and guilt and frustration, sorrow and relief and joy that divorce inspires in all of us. Take pride and gratitude in being a father. DO NOT SHAME YOURSELF because your marriage didn't work out. You will discover that you are still part of a family, just a different one!

2. Remember that divorce is between spouses, not parents and children. Continue to develop your relationship with your child. It may be more difficult, but be creative. Know that you can trust in your ability to let your child know that you love them, are there for them, and, most important, enjoy being with them.

3. You will now be developing a family system independent of your previous family. It will be different. Normalize your life with your child around your new routines.

4. Your child needs you and you need your child. As time goes on there will be many activities and adventures you will participate in with your child. School, sports, their friends, buying clothes, preparing meals—all the myriad of activities that help frame their lives from preschool to college.

5. Listen more closely to your child's feelings as you make the transition from a nuclear family to a new model of family life. Give your child the permission to feel whatever they are feeling with your

support. And take care of yourself. It will mean so much to your child to know that you can cope with the changes that lie ahead. It will reassure them that things will be manageable for them to know that their parents are stable. And remember the stability I am talking about is not about money and possessions, but in the heart and of the emotions.

For further self reflection and discussion:

1. Have there been any divorces in your family?

2. What about getting divorced is most frightening or upsetting for you?

3. What potential improvements may come for your child/children from divorce?

Jumping Rope

Your little worn canvas shoes are tossed on the floor
by the back door,
one white sock, one blue one lie abandoned nearby.

I think about all the jumping rope you have done in
these shoes,
all the 2:30-3:00 pm kindergarten afternoons we
wait for
your brother to get out of third grade and you
practicing
jumping rope.

Today part of me wants nothing to change;
I want you to be 5 years old forever,
for us to turn the rope together for
your friends and sing
"Cinderella dressed in yellow."

I know you are destined to
go out into the world
make a place for yourself,
and I know I will have helped you
learn to jump rope.

Kids, Dads and Education

An educational system isn't worth a great deal if it teaches young people how to make a living but doesn't teach them how to make a life. —Author Unknown

As September approaches and summer draws to an end, parents begin to prepare their children (and themselves) for school. I can still remember my son's first day at kindergarten, 25 years ago. Taking him to school, my wife and I were nervous as we reassured him that school would be fun. We often referred to Sesame Street and how Big Bird was afraid on the first day of school, too. We were proud as well as anxious about this important beginning and transition. All the parents escorted their children to the class, which would be in session from eight to twelve o'clock. The room was brightly decorated with craft projects, a large alphabet around the tops of all four walls, art easels and boxes of puppets and dress-up clothes. It really felt upbeat and fun! Then the parents went for coffee and tea with the principal in an assigned room. The principal reassured us that in his fifteen years of being principal of this school, every single parent had made it through the first day just fine!

Participating in school activities with my children, escorting field trips, being a room parent, being a helper in the class and assisting with school fairs and fund-raising have all been rich experiences for me as a father. They have helped me to feel as though I were a part of a community and have introduced me to many new friends I would not have otherwise met.

Aside from my eighth-grade, high-school and college graduations, I never saw my father or any other father that I can remember at school activities. I think my involvement with my own children has helped me to heal my own loneliness and longing for my father to show an interest in my activities. I also believe that my children have benefited enormously from my participation. School and all the activities associated with it take up an enormous amount of every child's life. The interest you show in what is a major part of their lives—a part that can also cause them worry and fear—comforts them by showing them that you care.

Participating in my children's schooling has let them know that I value their education, that school is important and that I make it a priority in my life. It has been reassuring for them to have a father who is familiar with the children in their class, and I believe that it has allowed them to feel more comfortable in school. I feel that my involvement in the early years of my children's education helped them feel more confident in school. In fact, research in the field of child development shows that there is a positive correlation between fathers' involvement in their children's education and their children's academic and social development.

Often times, in working with fathers in my psychotherapy practice, I find that dads have their hearts in the right place, but they may impress their children as too rigid in their desire to help. The dad's need to see his child be successful sometimes overshadows the needs of his child.

I consulted with our (then) fourteen-year-old son on this subject, and he gave me some interesting insights. Morgan thought that being supportive did not always mean helping out with the specifics of homework. He believed that listening to what he was doing and how he was doing it, without too much input, was most valuable. Mistakes would be there, but the overall experience of my interest and excitement about his work was better than helping with a lot of corrections. Great advice from a fourteen-year-old, certainly for dads of adolescents!

I have been very fortunate to have had the experience of being able to play an active role in my children's education. Many other fathers I know would like to be more involved but are prevented from doing so. For various reasons, fathers cannot always do all the things they would like to do for their children. Many questions arise: Where can sacrifices be made, what trade-offs can be made, and how much money can be given up for the time that would be gained? If parents work less and participate more in their children's early years, how does that affect their ability to save for their children's college years or provide for their own needs later in life?

I have found that it is simple to say that fathers should be more involved in their children's education, but many dads have difficulty arranging this. I am sure that all of the men who attend my programs for fathers would like to be able to spend more time with their children, especially in terms of involvement with their children's education. It appears to me that parents' economic class levels determine how much or how little they can be involved directly with their children. Self-employed professionals seem to have more flexibility than blue-collar workers or corporate employees, for example, while parents in management or ownership positions seem to be able to create more flexible hours. Society in general tends to discount fathers' interest in their children and to pay little attention to the difficulties they may have in balancing their work lives and their home lives.

No matter how busy their schedules are, parents need to rearrange them to allow some time each day to be with their children and to be their children's guides and mentors. Supporting children in their schoolwork and formal education is certainly an important area, but there are also many opportunities in day-to-day life for parents to share their knowledge and to educate their children. Reading to your child at night, looking at the newspaper together and going to movies and plays are all ways of bringing about stimulating discussions between you and your child. Parents have many unique experiences and interests, all of which can enrich their children's lives.

If possible, it's great to be involved at your child's school. Young kids, especially, love to see their dads at school. Last year I was a room parent for Julia's third-grade class and loved being an integral part of her day-to-day school life. Several other dads I know come regularly to help out in class. Field trips, school festivals and back-to-school nights are also opportunities to be part of your child's education in an important community, rather than academic, way.

Finally, express your interest in education by continuing to educate yourself. Attending lectures or classes, reading books and talking about your own new learning are powerful incentives for your children. Look for small opportunities to share educational experiences together. (Museums, art galleries and community centers are often good resources.)

For further self-reflection and discussion:

1. When you were growing up, what was your parents' attitude toward education?

2. How do you help prepare your child for school emotionally?

3. How can you participate in your child's education?

Crime and Punishment

Written after watching a father spank his child
vigorously at the San Francisco Academy of Science
in 1986 with my five year old son Morgan.
—Bruce Linton (journal notes)

Isn't there enough pain
for the time being?
I mean, how much anger
can a child handle?
Why do you
need to
punish
him?
What does a two-year-old do
that is
criminal?

Paternity and Peace

The real differences around the world today are not between Jews and Arabs; Protestants and Catholics; Muslims, Croats, and Serbs. The real differences are between those who embrace peace and those who would destroy it; between those who look to the future and those who cling to the past; between those who open their arms and those who are determined to clench their fists. —President Bill Clinton, 1997

Paternity and peace—people times feel these words are contradictory. Is the patriarchal model of Western society at the root of our international conflicts? Perhaps there is some degree of truth here, especially if we are to identify our images of what it means to be a man with the likes of John Wayne, Rambo, or the image created by the gladiator and so-called professional wrestling television shows.

If you look at the images of men presented by the media, what do you see? Violent heroes, murderers, rapists and assorted criminals make up much of the day-to-day reporting on men in the news as well as the casts of most television shows. Men featured in commercials usually alternate between the young macho-car-driving types and the incompetent males who can't do simple household chores.

I am surprised that more men and fathers don't take offense at these pejorative characterizations. In the mid 60's women began to respond to the stereotypes society had cast for them. Why haven't men followed suit in the 80's and 90's?

The issue of violence and world peace takes on new meaning when we become fathers, however. Many dads I have worked with talk about the apprehension they feel for their children in today's world. Thirty years ago parents worried that their kids might play hooky from school. Fifteen years ago parents worried about marijuana. Today's parents worry that their kids might be shot! The increase in school violence exemplified by the Columbine shootings has made many parents unsure about their children's basic daily safety.

Eric Erickson, the noted child psychiatrist, describes men who desire children as developing into the "generative" phase of psychosocial development. This developmental period is characterized by a greater and more profound interest in how the course of external events will effect the lives of others.

A special sense of compassion and social awareness is born with fatherhood. It seems almost biological in nature; so many new fathers appear to be vulnerable to events they might have ignored before they become dads.

This new "caring" opens the door for men to examine a deeper and more personal issue. As we encounter the difficulties and frustrations of understanding our new identities as fathers, we may experience feelings of anger and rage. Perhaps we had a father who expressed his anger in ways we think was destructive, yet we find ourselves imitating his behavior despite our good intentions. Maybe we had a physically abusive or alcoholic father, and now we can see how his behavior has influenced us. Our fathers' ability to understand and express anger and rage is the legacy we inherit as we become fathers.

How do we teach peace to our children? How can we help the world choose the path of peace rather than the path of war? As corny as it sounds, peace begins at home. When we as fathers understand our own anger and rage, we can begin to end this self-defeating lineage of violence that is passed on from generation to generation.

Joseph Chilton Pierce commented that it is not how many nuclear bombs we have that scares him, but rather who it is that can decide to push the button. It will be the next generation—our children—who are faced with the difficult decisions between peace and violence. Much of the knowledge they will use to choose between cooperation and conflict will come from their fathers.

For further self-reflection and discussion:

1. Be self-reflective; consider how you express your anger and frustration.

2. Do you think other men, especially dads, feel angry at times?

3. How do you calm yourself down when you get upset?

For Bob

This morning
I found myself thinking of us as two old trees,
you much taller than me.
Perhaps you would be a towering ancient redwood,
one who has reached across many years,
has watched the coming and goings
of jays and owls, squirrels and more
than a few beetles
whom you graciously coexisted with.
From the top of your tree
there would be a panorama.
I think you would watch with content the seasons
as they
passed and the rhythms
each changing one would bring.
You would feel the whole world around,
every passing day with the passions of spring, and
autumn,
winter and summer.

I think I might be an oak,
a California Scrub oak
built close to the ground.
I'd probably have more than a few broken branches
from not being flexible enough
when strong winds have come.
My roots would be secure,
deep in the earth, hidden.
I wouldn't be going anywhere.
I would be fed by the dark, rich soil.
My roots would grow as deep as they needed
to find water.

I too would have a nest or three in my branches,
crow or starling, owl or hawk.
I would enjoy their company,
happy to have them come
home to me each night.
I would have a few parasites burring in my bark:
beetles, lichen and moss. Over the years I
would probably have accumulated quite a collection.
I imagine we might be standing near each other,
having a conversation.
I would ask you when the last glimpse of sunset is
gone;
you would ask me if the morning dew
had evaporated from the grasses.
we would watch the season's metamorphosis,
we would look after each other.
Particularly on bad stormy days
we would be, just as we are,
good friends, each planted firmly in the soil
of this earth.

Materialism and the American Family

It is preoccupation with possessions, more than anything else, that prevents us from living freely and nobly. —Thoreau

Less than 100 years ago, 90% of the U.S. population lived on farms. Most were subsistence farms, with the family needing to work together to fulfill the physical necessities of life. The family was also the center for education and learning. Family values were what you learned in the day-to-day working-out of life: understanding the changing seasons and the best time to plant crops or a garden, being able to recognize a good horse, and how to get along with your neighbor. These were the necessities for survival, but they also connected us to a deeper rhythm of life within the environment and our communities. The Bible was a popular tool for teaching reading and for community guidance (i.e., "Do unto others as you would want them to do unto you"), but the majority of Americans were not orthodox in their religious practices. The value of teamwork and collaboration in both the family and community was the central value for survival and living a civilized life. The rural home was the center of American life and culture; it was the productive center of our society. The farm provided everything needed to live. Survival and success were vitally linked to our relationships with others. It could be said that the value of cooperation within the family and the community, and with the land, was the principal "family value" in America at the turn of the century.

Today, less than 3% of our population lives on farms. Almost all farms today are part of agribusiness. There are few subsistence farms. The home today is not a place of production but the center of consumption. Beginning in the 1920s, industrial development ejected the father from the house into the office or factory. Fifty years later, in the 1970s, just to "maintain" in our society of labor-saving devices and conveniences, mothers joined dads in the work force. The values of a consumer society, based mainly on materialism, slowly became the dominant values for American families.

The satisfaction once experienced in relationships with family members, friends and communities has been replaced by the illusion of satisfaction through owning things. It has become so desirable to have a new car, the fastest computer, the latest CD, the most fashionable clothes, that people believe they will find satisfaction in life by possessing them. Commercial advertising, through the use of sophisticated psychological techniques, attempts to sell us products that will make us believe we are part of the "good life." The price the American family has paid for the good life has led us to be a nation suffering from depression. We are lonely for each other and for a sense of being part of a greater community.

Many people today long for a sense of community and personal attachment. We live in isolation from friends and family, and the need or desire for cooperation and teamwork as a family value has been replaced by the value of independence and self-sufficiency (especially emotionally). This profound change in the function of the home, from a center of productivity and connection to one of consumerism, has taken its toll on all of us as parents and partners (husbands and wives) but has affected our children most profoundly. Frustrated children, either in school or day care; long hours of watching television; parents exhausted by trying to make ends meet—all of these have led us to our current discussion of family values in America.

Unfortunately, much of the family-values movement offers an oversimplified response to helping our families. There is the mistaken notion that if the fathers are out there making a "good living" and mothers are in the home caring for children, we will regain a sense of balance in our society. Some of the leaders in this new movement try to use the Bible as the ultimate authority on how we need to organize our families. I wish the solution was so easy—that we could just look up what we need to do in a book!

The family has been and is a dynamic living organism. It has changed and adapted in the course of history to many different configurations. It exists today in many different paradigms throughout the world. In America we need to look at our own unique cultural and social conditions and ask ourselves what our families need now.

What I propose is that, on the personal level—on the simplest level— we revitalize the family-farm value of cooperation. Like the couples who ran family farms, we as parents can begin to work together as partners, looking at the demands and chores of life much as the farm families did.

We need to ask how we can equitably share the tasks of sustaining a family. From earning our living to doing the laundry, we as parents can figure out how to navigate these tasks together. We can again learn how to reach out to our neighbors and friends, to help each other through the vicissitudes of modern life. We as families can learn to provide an environment in our daily lives that values cooperation and caring. We have to find the time, as families, to enjoy being together and sharing the events that shape our days. We want our children to be able to look to us, their parents, to have the skills and creativity to create a nurturing atmosphere.

The days of the father being at work and the mother staying home with the kids are gone, no longer a realistic model to emulate for parenting. As a family therapist, I often question whether it was ever the best model for raising children. But we have moved into new territory for parenting where, for both the satisfaction of the couple and survival of many families, men and women need to learn how cooperation and teamwork can lead to enjoyment and satisfaction in life.

For further self-reflection and discussion:

1. What is your response to the idea that family values are rooted in the cooperation between husband and wife?

2. What are three of the values that you and your partner convey to your children?

3. What will your child or children learn about family values from watching the relationship between you and your partner?

My Dad

It was mother I went to first when I cried
because she was there.
She took me to school and came to my kindergarten
graduation;
she made me lunches,
watched over me when I was sick.
She took me and my friends in her
blue 1953 Chevy convertible to the beach on Saturdays
as my father worked.
He got up at 5:30 in the morning;
he made sure we owned our house,
lived in a good neighborhood,
made certain we could buy new clothes,
bicycles, and go to summer camp.
He was the one who said
no choices but college.
I remember him smelling like chickens and newspapers
and trying to be an insurance salesman,
owing a liquor store until it got robbed too many
times.
Getting up early in the morning with him
smelling from Mennen Aftershave,
eating our breakfast together,
having coffee with lots of sugar in it
not knowing
he taught me so much about fatherhood
because he too
was there.

Father's Day

He didn't tell me how to live; he lived, and let me watch him do it.
—*Clarence Budington Kelland*

When we celebrate Father's Day, what are we celebrating? Is it a personal tribute to our fathers? Is it the commemoration of male parentage? Of all the holidays, Father's Day is one of the least observed and celebrated. Perhaps because men's relationships with their own fathers are often difficult, they feel reluctant to honor a day in their dads' behalf. In my work with fathers, I find that the number of men who want to honor their fathers on this day is equal to the number of men who want to mourn their relationships with their fathers. It seems that Father's Day is bitter-sweet national holiday, evoking both the admiration and disdain that men (and women) feel about their fathers.

As men become fathers themselves, celebrating this day can become very intense emotionally. I feel that men undervalue how profoundly they may be affected by this institutionalized ritual of acknowledging fatherhood. There is much denial in our society and in our personal lives about fatherhood. All men hope for fathers who can support them in both their physical and emotional needs. Young children want to trust the adults who are responsible for them. Parents are often not prepared or are not aware of how to "be there" for their kids.

The idea of a "Father's Day" came from Sonora Smart Dodd in 1910. She was raised by a single father who was a veteran of the Civil war. Her father was a generous and loving man. When she was in church one day listening to a sermon on Mother's Day she thought of the idea of Father's Day. It appears she intended Father's Day originally for June 5th but did not have enough time to get everything ready so June 19th became the official day.

Being there for your children means giving them your time and attention. Focusing on their needs and feelings, and helping children cope with their disappointments and excitements, is the core of parenting. This is true for fathers and mothers both!

It is not just having a male parent in the house that is important. What if we were to take Father's Day and Mother's Day and not identify them with gender?   It is the ability of the parent to be nurturing, warm and caring for his child. That is what fathering is all about. Today the American family is changing and developing. With Gay and Lesbian parents contributing to our matrix of parenthood. We may now understand it is the ability of the "parent" (male or female, gay, lesbian or transgender) to be nurturing and loving, understanding and patient committed to help the child find their way in the world that makes the difference and what we really honor on "Father's Day." It is time to see Father and Mother in a new way.

Many men can look back on their lives and find adults who were not their biological dads but who supported them, coached them, and were "mentor fathers." It is natural for children to seek out adults who can take pride in their achievements and convey to them that they are special and unique.

How men interact with their children and their mates, and how they feel about themselves as men, leaves a lasting impression on their children. Children's attitudes reflect the possibilities their parents see for themselves. Children learn the limitations of life and their own potential by watching how their parents deal with daily life—from how they greet the day to how they cope with disappointment and loss.

As we reflect on Father's Day this year, let us appreciate that, even if we were very wounded by our own fathers, we can be more substantial, more present in our children's lives than we felt our fathers were in ours. We can honor all the fathering influences who have contributed to our lives. We can dedicate ourselves on Father's Day to transforming the bond between ourselves and our families into a nurturing, cooperative and vital connection.

For Further self-reflection and discussion:

1.   What did you do for Father's Day last year?

2.   How was Father's Day celebrated when you were a child?

3.   Who would you like to acknowledge on Father's Day?

This Morning

This morning when I mediated
I reached the 9th level of Samadhi.
I encountered my own true Buddha nature;
I was not separate from any living being.

This afternoon I sat at the feet of
a great Sufi master.
I understood everything he said!
My eyes filled with tears.

Last night I made love to
three delicious women;
I was tender, moist and powerful.

This morning when I awoke
I was alone, tired, hungry and scared,
fabulous that nothing is permanent!

Christmas

One of the most glorious messes in the world is the mess created in the living room on Christmas day. Don't clean it up too quickly. —Andy Rooney

The holiday season creates a variety of feelings for families, from joy to dread. The pressures of our consumer society can make this a tense time of year. Crowded stores and traffic jams all add to the flurry of activity that often pushes us to the limits of our patience. We find ourselves asking the question, Is it really worth it? Could we do without this "holiday madness?" Couldn't we just skip the whole thing?

It is up to us as parents (or us as dads) to rescue Christmas from its commercialism and restore it as one of the special days in our children's lives. We can help create a special time of year to celebrate children, which I believe was the original intent of this holiday.

For most children, Christmas is not a religious holiday. Children don't associate a jolly fat man in a red suit with any religious symbolism. As my daughter once said, it is quite exciting to have a tree in the house. When our children were young, the surprise on their faces when they found their presents under the tree made it clear how special the experience was for them.

Christmas is a celebration of children. As I researched the history of St. Nick, I was led to his pre-Judeo-Christian past. It appears Santa Claus has his origins in a pre-Christian deity who was the protector of children, a nature spirit similar to the "green man" whose job it was to look out for the welfare of children. Both Hanukkah and Christmas may have been adjusted to coincide with this earlier folk tradition, which was the focus of the winter season.

Children, especially young ones, need to have special days that are just for them. Except for school graduations and religious ceremonies that mark memorable moments in their lives, children have few special days of their own. Only birthdays and Christmas remain as days truly reserved for kids. If these days are diminished in importance, children lose some of life's joy and the good feelings that go with it.

Santa Claus reaches out to children in a unique way. Presents and giving can certainly express love and good will at this time of year. Most children know Santa doesn't bring gifts to parents. Somehow, Santa Claus is just for them. For children who believe in the Santa Claus story, Christmas can be a magical time that brings much personal happiness.

Children who can experience the ancient myth of Santa Claus have their lives immensely enriched. The thought of a good, happy, colorfully dressed person who brings presents just for them creates a sense of magic in their lives. While difficulties and uncertainties in life are many, Christmas and the magic of Santa Claus help reassure children and give them a sense of hope. If our rational thinking forces us to deprive our children of the symbolic meaning that Santa represents, we lose the beneficial effects that can extend over the lifetime of the child.

Children have a need for magical thinking. From about four to ten years old, magical thinking actually helps kids cope with the world. The hardships, difficulties, even terrors that are part of our lives—which we cope with as adults—can be dealt with by young children through magical beliefs. Magical thinking declines as children grow and their rational consciousness is equipped to deal with the uncertainties and vicissitudes of life.

Together, my wife and I have tried to craft a unique Christmas for our children. We have a great time choosing a tree and decorating it. Our tree is covered with ornaments the kids have made over the years. Our children feel the joy of getting gifts that are given in celebration of them, with no one but Santa to thank.

As our children have gotten older, we have begun to explore the meaning of "peace" at this time of year. This is a time when we can all wish for a world that is more nurturing and peaceful. Our children can begin to express the feelings of gratitude that reflect their own experience of Christmas and what it means to them. Also, they now realize that it was Dad or Mom, Grandpa or Grandma that loved them enough to buy this present for them. They do express their appreciate now for the many "Santa Clauses" that visit them each year.

The winter solstice, the seasonal change, begins to mark a time of turning inward. With less daylight, the cold, the change in the landscape around us, we all feel some of the seasonal transition. Connecting with these changes is part of the experience of Christmas for us, too. My wife and I take pleasure in creating a meaningful time for us to enjoy being a family together.

For further self-reflection and discussion:

1. What do you find most difficult about the holiday season?

2. How did your family celebrate Christmas when you were a child?

3. How would you like to celebrate Christmas, and how can you talk about it with your partner?

Ode to Canadian Geese

when there is no time for poetry
and life is all doing
no being
I watch the Canadian Geese
who graze with their mates on the grass near my
house
they have only a short distance to fly
to reach the bay
and glide so gently
on the silent water

Chapter 20

Food for Thought

We think fast food is equivalent to pornography, nutritionally speaking. —Steve Elbert

Educating ourselves about parenting is a critical part of our being "good enough" fathers. Understanding the importance of food and the need for independence among small children is basic to helping them develop good eating habits and self-esteem.

Many of the difficulties I see with dads of teenagers and families with adolescents are issues that began in early childhood as struggles around food. As a family therapist, one of the areas I want to discuss when a family comes in for treatment is its food and eating routines.

For young children, how often and how much they eat can vary greatly. Young children's appetites are not organized around the adults' defined eating times. As adults we have learned—as children do over time—to be organized around eating three times a day. Our external and internal rhythms are now structured around these times. Young children are much more internally focused. A three-year-old can want nothing to eat at noon and by twelve-thirty be famished. A young child focusing on play may find lunchtime (and food) an unwelcome intrusion.

Young children's need for independence is often met with great ambivalence. Eating is a way they may experiment with this confusion. Acting out around food is one way a young child tries to understand and master his need for independence and autonomy. What he puts in his mouth and how much he eats and when he eats are among the few ways he can exercise independent control in his life. Children can eat huge meals one day and not be hungry at all the next. They can love a special food one week and refuse to eat it a week later. Sometimes a child may want to be totally catered to, while at other times the same child may want to be left alone.

While all dads would like their children to enjoy eating, each parent brings his or her own hang-ups to this area. Usually there are unresolved issues from our own childhood that we react to in our children. If you remember your own past experiences around eating, you need not continue them with your children. Forcing a child to eat is a certain road to eating problems. In order for a child to enjoy eating, he or she must be in control to some degree.

Toddlers will often use food to test limits. They will always want the food you don't have. You can let your child know that "This is what we have for dinner tonight. We will have [whatever the child is asking for] tomorrow night." Parents need to learn to relax around meal times. Children's nutritional needs are fairly simple, and you are probably doing just fine if your child falls within the normal ranges for weight and height and if the available food is generally nutritious.

If you haven't made food a struggle for both you and your children, by the time they are four or five they will find it exciting to try new foods and experiment with new tastes. Establishing independence about eating is one way in which we help our children learn their own limits and foster their ability to make their own choices, an essential ingredient in positive self-esteem. Pickiness, refusal of certain foods, wide variation in tastes from one week to the next, these are all part of the normal phases kids go through. Tolerance is what we need to learn—and show—as parents.

Of course, if your child refuses to eat over a prolonged period or is very thin or overweight, it would be appropriate to seek your doctor's advice.

Respecting our children's need for control, and being aware of our own eating history, we can proceed into the future with our families in a relaxed and positive manner at meal times. I hope this has been some food for thought.

For further self-reflection and discussion:

1. What are the "feeling tones" at your meals? Tense or relaxed?

2. How flexible or rigid are you about your child's eating?

3. When you were growing up, what were the rules about food and eating? What was the mood around the dinner table with your parents?

The Heart Donkey

it was only because
my stubbornness
was strong enough
that i have been able
to travel so far

Learning from Special-Needs Children

Life is a succession of lessons which must be lived to be understood. —Helen Keller

The United States today is not a society that is supportive of parents or family life. Although politicians and television commercials would like us to believe otherwise, social connectedness, childcare support and sharing parental information are all very difficult for anyone who has children. The problem is compounded by our jobs, which ask us to compartmentalize our lives so we are parents at home and employees at work—as if one is not influenced by the other. Mix all the ingredients together in the best of all circumstances, and one must still continually seek creative alternatives to meet the challenges of parenting.

These challenges are increased exponentially for parents of special-needs children. Due to accidents or genetic or birth problems, these children develop and grow at a different pace than what is rather arbitrarily considered normal.

There are many challenges that greet the fathers of special-needs kids. Our socialized emphasis on competition is normally manifested in our desire to have our children meet our needs for success. Fathers of special-needs children, however, have the opportunity to free themselves of preconceptions and expectations and to learn what their children have to offer in other ways. Though the process may be painful and difficult, the evolution of this unconditional love is as great a gift to the father as to the child.

At a conference I attended many years ago a woman shared a story about how much she and her husband had wanted a child. Since they had medical problems that did not permit conception, they decided to adopt. They were both successful in their careers and had set up their lives to indulge themselves with their child. The woman spoke of what they had planned—the traveling, the classes in art and music, and the books they would share with their child.

But soon they noticed that he appeared to be developing more slowly than their friends' children, and it was discovered that he had Down Syndrome. Tears came to the woman's eyes as she spoke. She said her son is now 30 years old and a wonderful, loving person. She talked about how difficult it was for her and her husband to give up their hopes for what might have been and to discover the very different and special child who had come into their life for them to love.

Special-needs children teach us all that loving our children is not about who we want them to be, but about who they are.

For further self-reflection and discussion:

1. How is your child different from how you hoped he/she might be?

2. What do you love most about your child?

3. How are you different from what your parents had hoped for in you and your life?

For Phyllis

Everyone worries about the future.
If we can be here now,
in this moment,
the past and the future join together.
It is all we need,
the present.
We take our time
walking the hills of Marin
or the coast by Stinson beach.
We have coffee,
talk about our work, family and friends.
It seems so routine,
as if not much happens,
but in our conversations together
the world unfolds itself
to us
eternally.

Chapter 22

The Five Myths of Fatherhood

You don't really understand human nature unless you know why a child on a merry-go-round will wave at his parents every time around and why his parents will always wave back. —W.D. Tammeus

If you're like most new or expectant dads, you probably have a few assumptions about what it means to be a father. Those ideas are rooted in your experiences with your own father and in what you believe society expects of fathers. Unfortunately, few resources exist to help men address these issues or put common myths to the test. Yet the more you examine and understand your unspoken expectations of fatherhood, the better chance you have of becoming the parent you want to be or that your child needs.

Perhaps the biggest myth of all is that there's only one definition of a "good father." There isn't. You'll craft your own idea of what it means to be a father in a way that meets your needs and the needs of your family—and you'll do it over time. Here are five other commonly held myths:

Myth 1: Only the expectant mother's feelings are important

Your partner's amazing body changes during pregnancy, and the focus on the birth process makes it easy to think that her feelings are the only ones that count. Your concern for her physical and mental health is important now and during the postpartum period, but so are your own feelings. It's easy for an expectant dad to talk excitedly about the positives of becoming a father. It's much tougher to give voice to the equally important—and inevitable—feelings of fear and apprehension. Will I faint at the birth? Will there be medical complications? How will our relationship change? Can I pursue my career and also be the father I want to be?

Your partner needs to hear your feelings, and you need to give voice to them. Many men keep their fears about pregnancy and fatherhood to themselves because they don't want to add to their partner's worries. Don't be afraid of burdening her. Most women crave this kind of interaction, and they know that becoming a father brings challenges. Sharing your fears with your wife or partner will bring you closer.

You can also seek out other expectant fathers, read a good book about becoming a father, and attend a fathering class or group for support. Give yourself permission to express both your feelings of vulnerability and excitement. By voicing your concerns during pregnancy and early parenting, you challenge the myth that only your partner's feelings are important and lay the foundation for becoming an actively involved dad.

Myth 2: Newborns don't really need their fathers

The intense connection between your partner and infant, especially if they're breastfeeding,   can leave you wondering whether your baby really needs you. Rest assured he does. You're an important person in his life, and being with you is comforting and soothing to him. To bond with your baby, hold, rock, and coo at him, but wait until after he eats so you'll have his full attention. Taking over after a meal also gives your partner a chance to recoup her energy after breastfeeding.

You can help feed your baby if your partner expresses milk into a bottle or if you decide to supplement or replace breastfeeding with formula feeding. And you can help your baby indirectly by helping your partner around the house. Lightening her workload is nurturing for her and allows her more relaxed time with the baby. Remember, you make a difference to the whole family.

Myth 3: Men don't know how to care for young children

This is a great lie that keeps fathers from having a close relationship with their babies and causes unnecessary anxiety for new mothers who fear that men aren't capable of handling newborns. Even Dr. Spock, the late pediatrician and best-selling author, cautioned in his first book that men are subject to "clumsiness" around babies. He changed his opinion in subsequent editions, and you should, too. We know now that a father can be a child's primary caregiver. Parenting is learned on the job by everyone, moms and dads both. If you spend time with your baby, you'll become sensitive to his needs. To make certain that happens, send your partner out of the room sometimes or choose a childcare task that's yours alone. Let her know you're capable of handling things.

Chapter 23

Myth 4: Men who focus on their children can't make it in the work world

Men are raised to value work as their main source of worth and self-esteem. Society's underlying message is that men who make sacrifices and choose family over career advancement do it because they can't succeed at work. But we're at the beginning of a huge shift in cultural norms. More men are finding parenthood meaningful, and that's raising the status of fathers. Some men are trading career advancement for time with their family because they value the fulfillment they find in fatherhood, not because they can't hack it in the job market. More men than ever feel that being a good father is a significant accomplishment in life and are choosing to make it a priority because they want to.

Myth 5: You're destined to be just like your own father

Your father will take on new significance when you become a dad. It's natural to reflect on your history and think that, for better or worse, you'll follow in your father's footsteps. But your own father needn't be your primary role model for parenting. He's just one influence on what kind of dad you'll become. Look to others who have nurtured you over the years, including teachers, coaches, friends, uncles, brothers, and so on, and create your own identity as a father.

In my research throughout the world, I've found no evidence of one consistent model for fatherhood. Different cultures approach fatherhood in a variety of ways. In fact, in some African cultures, "father" is a group of men, not an individual. In each culture, fatherhood means something different. For our fathers, being a good father meant providing the family with a home, food, and education. Our own dads probably didn't spend as much time with us as we would like to spend with our own children. But they did what they thought was best for us, given societal and family demands at the time.

You, too, must make choices that are best for your family. Try to see fatherhood as a role you grow into as you explore the possibilities. You can take the positives from your own family history and add to them in ways that never occurred to your own father.

How to challenge the five myths of fatherhood:

1. Take time to reflect on how becoming (or being) a father is affecting you. Share your feelings with your partner and other new and expectant fathers.

2. Hold, rock, and talk to your newborn right from the birth.

3. Learn how to change diapers, give baths, feed your baby, and be part of his daily life.

4. Consider what career compromises you are willing to make to spend time with your child. This is an experiment that takes place over time.

5. Take what you like best about your father, teachers, coaches, friends, and relatives to create your own identity as a dad. Anyone who has nurtured you can be a good role model.

For Morgan

Love and treat yourself well.
Make mistakes.
Get your heart broken once or twice
(at least).
Risk everything if you believe in your cause.
Let your experience be your teacher.
Don't be afraid of bad times
(they find us all).
Anger and frustration are your friends,
aggression a close cousin.
Loneliness is unavoidable;
seek solitude to restore yourself.
Know you will always have poetry.
Sometimes it will make sense,
at other times be obscure.
I am proud and fortunate to be your father.
Your creativity and caring have been a great gift;
you have enriched my soul beyond your knowing.
Let this poem
remind you of our bond,
like the warmth of the morning sun
greeting you and reminding you
another day has arrived:
with endless possibilities.

The Three Trimesters of Pregnancy for Men

The First Trimester of Pregnancy for Men

Congratulations, your partner (and you) are now pregnant! Your baby is beginning its life inside the womb. All the care and nurturing your baby needs is happening in your partner's belly! The transition to parenthood and becoming a father is slowly starting to take hold of you. You're going to be a dad...Yikes!—Wow!—Incredible! What should you expect during this first trimester? Most men have a positive reaction to finding out about the pregnancy, but they may also have doubts and confusion. An unplanned pregnancy can begin with feelings of ambivalence. For expectant fathers pregnancy seems to stimulate feelings of both fear and hope. Understanding your feelings during this time can help you begin to see how your role from "man to dad" is developing.

Common anxieties in the first trimester are fears about your partner's health, worries about money, and concerns about what type of father you will be. In the first few months, as your partner's body adjusts to the pregnancy she may experience morning sickness, sleeplessness, mood swings, fatigue and changes in eating habits. Although these symptoms are normal, you may not be use to seeing your wife this uncomfortable. You may wonder what you can do to help. Many expectant dads start to look ahead and feel worried about how having a baby will affect their finances. If both you and your partner have been working, you may begin to think about how you will be affected by the change in income if your wife will be off work for a while. Concerns about the need for a larger house, a new car or how to anticipate what new expenses you will have once the baby has arrived are common anxieties in the early stages of pregnancy.

Finally, many expectant fathers are concerned about what type of father they will be.

You may begin to think about what it was like for your father when you were born. How prepared was your dad when he became a father? What opportunities do you feel you have as an expectant dad that your father didn't? All these new "anxieties" are the normal feelings that are "stirred-up" by finding out that you will be a father in less than a year. In our society we don't make many accommodations for expectant dads. We are not sure what they need and what their role should be during pregnancy. It has been my experience that the sooner expectant dads can be involved, the more included they will feel in their new "family." Going to the doctor's visits with your partner, talking with other fathers, beginning to look at a few of the new books on parenting are all ways to begin your transition to parenthood.

Here are here are a few practical tips that pregnant dads have shared with me during the First Trimester of pregnancy.

For your wife/partner:

- Talk with your wife about the hopes and dreams, fears and anxieties, of having a child together.

- Make time to regularly go on walks together.

- Talk about how your lives can slow down, how you can both do less in the coming months and enjoy the pregnancy.

For yourself:

- Choose the friends you want to share the news about "being pregnant."

- Go to a bookstore and look through the books on parenting.

- Take time alone to reflect on your feelings about becoming a father.

The Second Trimester of Pregnancy for Men

In the second trimester you will have a chance to hear your baby's heartbeat and possibly see your baby through ultrasound. These experiences usually bring a heightened sense of reality...we are really going to have a baby!

In our society we tend to value men's financial contributions to our families more than our emotional contributions. It is understandable then why concerns over money or financial security become the focus of many expectant fathers. It may also become an acceptable "male" way of expressing concern for your partner and unborn child. It is usual to begin to think about how your finances will be changed by having a baby, but if you become preoccupied with money concerns, something deeper may be troubling you. If you feel that dealing with "the money" is all your responsibility it may be touching on deeper issues of competency or security. It is important in this second trimester to discuss your finances with your partner but also to keep them in perspective. Developing a little "tolerance for uncertainty" is a useful skill both in pregnancy and parenthood.

Many expectant dads report that during the second trimester there is a change in the sexuality with their partners. Each expectant mom will respond differently to the hormonal changes her body is going through. For some women pregnancy can intensify their sexual arousal, while for others it appears to diminish it. As a father-to-be it is important to see that in this second trimester many of your partner's responses may be driven by the changes her body and hormones are putting her through. At this point in the pregnancy you may begin to feel concerned about how your relationship with your partner is fluctuating. You may begin to notice how the routines you have taken for granted are changing. Couples often share basic routines around meals, leisure time and household chores. A simple habit, like a Sunday morning breakfast, may no longer be desirable to your partner if she has morning sickness. If you both used to enjoy going out weekend evenings and now she feels too fatigued, how are you going to respond? You may feel disappointed to discover the partner you felt you knew and understood and depended on is no longer herself. Every couple experiences these changes differently. Try and talk with your partner about the changes your feel the relationship is going through. Try and be understanding with each other about all the happiness, guilt, anticipation, ambivalence and frustration that is now going on in your lives. Establishing a pattern of open communication with your partner at this time in the pregnancy will allow the both of you to move toward the birth in a more supportive and positive relationship.

Here are here are a few practical tips that pregnant dads have shared with me during the Second Trimester of pregnancy.

For your wife/partner:

- Start to take-on more of the chores around your house or apartment.

- Let your partner know she is going to be a great mom.

- Let your wife know that you and she can talk about both the positive and negatives about being   pregnant.

For yourself:

- Talk with two other new fathers about how they are feeling as parents.

- If possible, ask your father what it was like for him when you were born.

- Go for a walk with a friend who will listen to you talk about how you feel about being a "pregnant" dad.

The Third Trimester of Pregnancy for Men

The last three months of pregnancy have begun. Within 90 days your baby will join you and your partner on the "outside." Your partner's body is making the final adjustments in getting ready for labor and your baby is beginning to mature in preparation for birth. You may have finally adjusted to "being pregnant" when a new flood of feelings arise within you as you get ready to welcome your baby to the world.

You've probably begun to wonder what you will be like as a father. What are the expectations of this new role as a parent? Reflecting on your father as a model may not fit how you see yourself as a dad. Fatherhood from generation to generation has changed significantly. The social and societal expectations for fathers, even twenty years ago, are quite different from what they are today. Fathering and parenthood are not fixed roles. Dads' roles are influenced by the society in the time when they live and the needs of each individual family.

Thinking about your own father and his parenting is a good place to start. What did you most enjoy about your father? What will you do different? Do you see any of your friends or family members who you feel are fathering the way you would like to? This last trimester is a good time to re-examine your relationship with work and think about how you may want to make adjustments before, for and after the birth. Remember to allow yourself flexibility in your planning. No one can anticipate exactly what it will be like when their baby arrives, and the best- made plans often need to adjust to circumstances and feelings you cannot be aware of before the baby has arrived.

Being involved in a prenatal class is a way to prepare yourself for the birth. More important, when you take a prenatal class with your partner you can begin to prepare as a couple to share the birth experience. What will be your role during birth? What are your partner's expectations? Can you allow yourself to think about what you may need? Classes will give you the understanding of the stages of the birth process and what to expect during labor and delivery.

The physical changes your partner has been going through will intensify during the last trimester. These physical changes will also have an effect on her psychological state. As men, there is nothing parallel for us as to the bodily hormonal changes a woman undergoes during pregnancy. The enthusiasm she may have experienced in the second trimester as the pregnancy was beginning "to show" does not guarantee she will feel the same way in the last month, when she has the full weight of the baby inside her. Expectant mothers can feel out of control of their bodies and this can be a very frightening experience.

You may feel some distress at your partner's needs for increased help during the final month. No matter how much a couple can do in preparing for the birth of their baby, or getting their home ready for its arrival, there are always a few things that feel incomplete. Be patient with each other. Remember to keep the channels of communication open, neither of you can know exactly what birth and parenthood will be like. If you feel overwhelmed between work and getting ready for the baby, it would be wise to talk about this with your partner. This is a good time to reach out for support. Other dads have gone through what you are experiencing. Friends, family, the dads in your prenatal class, other dads whom you may work with can all be sources of support for you.

Here are here are a few practical tips that pregnant dads have shared with me about the Third Trimester of pregnancy.

For your wife/partner:

- Get "the nest" ready together if possible. Work together getting things for your baby, such as baby furniture, getting the house ready, preparing extra meals.
- Find out how you can view at least two birth films together.
- Let your wife know that you want to know what you can do to "be there" for her at the birth.
- Go on a tour of where your baby will born.

For yourself:

- Begin to plan for the birth. Check and see how flexible you work will be both about time off for birth and after.
- Ask two new fathers about their experience of their baby's births.
- Reach out to the men in your childbirth preparation class; see if you can have a dads-to-be night out.
- Find an exercise program that you feel you could continue after the baby is born.

The First Twelve Months of Fatherhood

The First Month of Fatherhood

Welcome to your first month of fatherhood! You have arrived home from the hospital proud, excited and perhaps a bit exhausted from the experience of childbirth. What's next?

Preparing for birth is all-consuming and most expectant fathers don't think too much about what happens after they get home with their wife and new baby. The birth experience creates intense emotions. You have a new sense of yourself. You are not just a man, but a father! The pregnancy and birth are the beginning of a lifelong journey of becoming a parent and being a dad. You will need the next few months, perhaps the whole next year, to comprehend your new role.

Most of today's dads are needed, right from day one, to be involved in caring for their new baby. Both moms and dads usually have full time jobs today. As women are contributing more to the financial stability of the family, dads are contributing more to childcare and chores at home.

Keep in mind that the first month with your baby at home is an amazing experience. There are a million new things to learn! A baby needs pretty much 24-hour supervision. You can learn with your wife all the baby basics. Changing diapers, holding and bathing your baby, supporting your wife in her breast feeding or sharing in bottle feedings, doing these things together will help you both begin to feel secure in caring for your newborn and help develop good communication with your wife. Remember for first-time parents it is "on-the-job" training. Give yourselves permission not to know everything.

We have been raised as men to "be in control," we were supposed to know how to "solve the problems," but as a new father we need to be able to give ourselves permission not to know all the answers. Just as our baby is slowly learning to adjust to the world outside his mother's womb we need to allow time for ourselves to learn and adapt to our new role as a father.

Remember that your wife's body will be adjusting to the hormonal changes of childbirth, and that moodiness and irritability are not to be taken personally. I am surprised at how few fathers know this. Keep in mind that by supporting your wife you are helping your baby too!

Here are here are a few practical tips that new dads have shared with me to get the most out of your 1st month of fatherhood.

For your baby:

- Learn how to comfortably hold your baby. To burp your baby hold her securely against your shoulder and gently rub or pat his back.

- Communicate with your baby. Hold your baby in your lap and look into her eyes, speak or   sing softly to your baby.

For your wife/partner:

- See that you have a comfortable chair for your wife to nurse the baby in.

- Tell your wife how proud you are of her. Let her know she is doing great as a mom.

For yourself:

- Help burp the baby after feedings and "hang out" with her.

- Talk with you wife about how much company or how many family visitors you want in the first month. Remember to put yourselves first; you and your wife need time and privacy to get comfortable with your new baby and being a family.

- Don't be embarrassed by what you don't know. How could you know it! All that matters is that you have the desire and interest to learn and develop.

The Second Month of Fatherhood

Congratulations, you're at the second month fatherhood! Your adventure is underway! The first month of fatherhood is occupied by adjusting to your new situation, such as the changes in your schedule and routines, settling into how and when your baby needs to be fed, changing diapers and giving baths, trying to get enough sleep, and communicating with your wife in your new roles as parents.

Many new fathers comment on how wonderful and difficult that first month is. Your baby is still small and helpless but by the second month you may feel a difference as you hold him. He may seem to be more of a person.

In the first month, like you, he was just adjusting to his new situation, now the difference between waking and sleeping is more defined. Your baby is much more active and alert when he is awake. Your baby is starting to observe more about the world around him. As his father you may also begin to notice the changes he is able to perceive. Your baby can probably tell the difference between you and your wife. He can deepen his attachment to you as you hold and soothe him. Perhaps you are able to distinguish whether he is crying because he needs food or because he needs a diaper changed, or has gas.

You may find yourself feeling very stretched by trying to balance both family and work responsibilities. There will probably be times when neither home nor work is getting enough of your time. It may even feel as if it will always be like this. Be patient over time and as your baby grows and you and your wife gain more confidence in your parenting you'll find how to make the adjustments you need to make in order to feel less overwhelmed by your changing schedule. You and your wife may find that if you just surrender to your baby's schedule, especially in the evenings, it may reduce the tension that is created when you try to get a two-month-old baby to bed "on time."

Here are here are a few practical tips that new dads have shared with me to get the most out of your second month of fatherhood:

For your baby:

- Continue to hold your baby as much as possible. Find time when you can be with your baby without distractions.

- With your wife, the two of you together give your baby a bath. Talk about what your baby seems to need to make him comfortable getting   washed.

For your wife/partner:

- Tell your wife what you appreciate about her "mothering."

- Find time when you can take the baby and she can take time just for herself.

For you:

- Talk about the change you are experiencing in trying to balance work and family life with your wife and friends.

- Try to find other new dads to talk with about the transition to parenthood. Often you can contact the men who were in your prenatal class or friends who might be willing occasionally to share their experiences of fatherhood.

The Third Month of Fatherhood

In the third month of fatherhood you begin to hope for a "routine" to be established for your baby. But that's not always the case! It doesn't mean anything is "wrong" with your baby or that you and your wife are not doing things right. Babies take a long time to adjust to being in the outside world. Remember, for nine months your baby's every need was met on demand. Eating, sleeping, all bodily functions were met immediately and without any effort while inside the womb. Over the last two months your baby has been learning how to communicate her needs to you. Needs she doesn't even understand herself.

Dads at this time often hit the "exhaustion point." The unpredictability of the nights is usually the toughest. Not getting continual nights' sleep leaves many new fathers feel spent and fatigued. Along with being physically overtired, new dads need to recognize how emotionally weary they have become making all the adjustments to their new lifestyle. I remember how I felt when we went out as a family; it was my wife, our baby and their pack animal, me...carrying all our stuff that we now needed to take with us.

At three months the roles of mother and father can become polarized. Dad spends less time with baby and mom spends more. Dads may feel they can't calm the baby as easily as their wife probably can. Research has shown that whoever, mom or dad, spends more time with baby gets to know their needs better. But it is also clear that babies need both their fathers and mothers.

Your baby is now learning that your hands are larger and hold him differently than do his mom's. Father's cloths feel different and he has a different smell than mother does. He can feel the differences of your skins and recognize the differences of your voices. These experiences, that there are two different kinds of people in the world who both care for him and love him, is very important. We now know the care and stimulation of the father at this early age sets in motion a developmental process for later learning.

By staying involved in the early months of your child's life you are preparing your child for the future. Involved fathers help stimulate better social skills and problem-solving abilities in their children, skills that often show up years later. So even if you are wearing a bit thin in this third month of fatherhood.... hang in there!

Here are a few practical tips that new dads have shared with me to get the most out of your third month of fatherhood.

For your baby:

- Babies are discovering their own hands and are fascinated by them. Hold your baby on your lap and let him grasp your finger.

- Your baby may like to sit contentedly and look at things. Have a safe place, a crib, playpen or infant seat, that won't tip over where you can place objects for your baby to look at. From time to time change the views your baby has of the objects she's been viewing.

For your wife/partner:

- Take a walk together as a family. See if you can have the baby in a "front pack" that is on you.

- Talk with your wife about each of you getting twenty minutes to yourselves in the evening.

For you:

- Find time to walk with the baby by yourself. Use this time to appreciate how by caring for your baby you are making a very important contribution to her life.

- See if you can leave work ten or fifteen minutes early and have a cup of coffee of tea by yourself.

The Fourth Month of Fatherhood

Having a baby and making the transition to parenthood is a very complicated process. I say this from both my professional perspective as a family counselor, and my own experience as a father of two children. With all the various pressures on young families, often there is not enough time or energy for parents to have the sexual contact one or both partners want.

During the fourth month you start to notice that there is a change in your sexual relationship with your wife. It is very normal for this to happen, but why this happens is not well understood by dads. The reduced sexual desire experienced by new mothers is linked to a natural hormonal process. For the survival of young babies the mother's attention and emotional energies are totally focused on the infant. This "preoccupation" with the baby is part of our biological heritage for the survival of the species! In fact, biologically, new mothers secrete a hormone that reduces their sexual desire. So, if your wife feels sexually withdrawn from you but too concerned about your baby... things are going well!

It is normal for new dads in the early months of fatherhood to feel jealous of their new babies. Perhaps it is really not jealousy of their babies, but a feeling stemming from the loss of attention they feel from their wife. This is probably a normal response to the wife's feeling of "preoccupation" with the baby.

The period of the pregnancy is usually an emotionally close time for a couple. The intensity of the pregnancy and early months of parenting now give way to the daily needs of the baby being the center of the relationship. As a new dad you begin to wonder when your "couple" relationship will get back to the way it use to be. There is good news and bad news at this point. The bad news is that the relationship can never go back to the way it "use to be." The good news is with time and patience your relationships as a "couple" can become more intimate and satisfying.

A natural maturing of the sexuality and intimacy occurs as you make the adjustments and changes as partners and parents. A mutual respect and appreciation can develop within the couple for each other as individuals. It is difficult for us as men if our experience of intimacy is linked only to our sexuality. For many new dads the early months of fatherhood provide a challenge to expand their feelings about intimacy. Many new dads find it difficult to talk about sexuality with their wives. I encourage you to talk about the sexuality in your relationship with your wife. As you go through life as a parent and adult there may be many conversations you have with your wife about the changing sexuality in your relationship.

Here are a few practical tips that new dads have shared with me to get the most out of your fourth month of fatherhood.

For your baby:

- Your baby may discover that she can begin to make sounds. You can make sounds with your baby and see which one she responds to.

- Your baby is enjoying trying to hold things. See which toys he likes to hold most. Over the next few months he may try to pass the object from one hand to the other.

For your wife/partner:

- Discuss the changes you are experiencing in your sexuality with your wife.

- Respect how much your life has changed in the last four months! Talk about how parenthood is an opportunity to develop a deeper feeling of closeness, although life seems so stressful at times.

For yourself:

- Take time to get a massage and sauna.

- Take a walk with a friend and let him know what you have discovered about being a father.

The Fifth Month of Fatherhood

Becoming a father changes the way we view ourselves and the world around us. We see ourselves less as a son in relation to our own parents and more on equal footing with our own father. During the first year of parenthood it is usual for a new father to reflect on how he was raised by his own father.

In the new fathers' groups I have lead the dads usually feel "bitter sweet" when talking about their own fathers. Most of the dads express how they wish their own fathers had spent more time with them. Many of them also see that their dads were very dedicated to the family but expressed it in working and providing economically for the family. Dad as "breadwinners" has been the prominent role model for fatherhood in the last fifty years. As we discuss our fathers in the group, many dads reflect on how being the economic provider was the way their father showed his love. Yet, men long for a father who would have been more emotionally warm and available to them. New dads wonder how much of the role modeling of fatherhood they have "inherited" from their dads.

From the research I've done it appears that fatherhood is socially constructed. What that means is that fathers usually adapt themselves to the needs of the family and community at their particular time in history. On the other hand, motherhood has been a stable role model, particularly in the early months of parenthood. Almost universally mothers are seen as the primary caregivers of young children. With most mothers working, dads play a greater role in the nurturing and care of young children.

We are seeing a transition in the role of fatherhood; dads are now involved in the early years of parenting and continue to play an equal role with mothers as children grow up. This change has come about, in part, because in today's society both mothers and fathers are working. Women want work to be a meaningful part of their lives and find creative satisfaction in their careers. Fathers, not just out of necessity, but out of desire, want to be involved in meeting the daily needs in their children's lives. It appears that for new fathers, parenthood is an important part of their identity as men. No longer do fathers want to be defined only by their work, jobs, or careers. Today, fatherhood involves caring for their children and a desire to enjoy their families as part of the creativity in their lives. Fatherhood for men has become central to finding satisfaction and meaning in life. Enjoy the adventure in your fifth month of fatherhood.

Here are a few practical tips that new dads have shared with me to get the most out of your fifth month of fatherhood.

For your baby:

- Your baby will enjoy playing "peek-a-boo" with you.

- Get a bottle of soap bubbles and see if your baby enjoys watching you blow bubbles.

For your wife/partner:

- Find 5 minutes a day to talk about how the day went for your wife and you.

- Plan a video "film festival." You might enjoy comedies about family life, right about this time.

For yourself:

- If you can, ask your father what he has enjoyed and what has been difficult for him as a father.

- Ask a male friend about his relationship with his father.

- If you have a brother or sister ask them to describe to you how they understand your father.

The Sixth Month of Fatherhood

You've been a dad for half a year now and "on-the-job" training is starting to pay off. You can feel more confident and experienced in how you approach your baby's needs. Check-in with yourself, are you feeling satisfied with your participation in caring for your baby? Do your new responsibilities as a father seem like chores or do you find pleasure in being able to care for your baby?

Is there tension between you and your wife? It is usual for couples to find, at six months, that they have tension that has built up around how the scheduling is organized. Since your baby keeps changing, it is difficult to have a "regular routine." Many new dads find that between home life, work and getting enough sleep...it just can't be done. Tension can build between you and your partner as she has differing needs about how and when things should happen.

It is important to remember that both you and your partner grew up in very different families. Each of us, as parents, expects our partner to understand how we want to do things with our baby. From feedings to naps, getting the dishes done or the baby to sleep, with all these tasks we usually expect our partners to know the "right" way to do them.

As a marriage therapist I usually try and help couples at the sixth month to understand that it is normal for each partner to have a way that they want to have things done or organized that is very different from their partner. It often seems frustrating that your partner doesn't understand what you see as so obvious. It is a very important time for both mothers and fathers to understand that they can work together to find the unique way that they will do things in their family together.

You may find that your baby is getting ready for solid food or that a tooth is starting to come in. Just when you get comfortable with a routine...something changes! Tolerance for change is the key survival skill as a dad and a partner at this sixth month.

Here are a few practical tips that new dads have shared with me to get the most out of your sixth month of fatherhood.

For your baby:

- Notice how your baby can express a wide range of feelings: anger, joy, frustration, excitement, curiosity, frustration. Watch your baby's expressions and see if you can understand what he is feeling.

- Your baby can focus much more and when you play together she can respond to your playfulness and excitement. Investigate a stationary walker so your baby can try standing and bouncing.

For your wife/partner:

- Talk with your wife about the different "styles" of parenting you experienced as children. Conclude your discussion with a commitment to work out the way you will work as a team, together, in the family you have started.

- Ask your wife to talk with you about what she loves and hates about being a mother for six months. Share the positive and negatives you have learned about fatherhood.

For yourself:

- Make sure you are eating well and exercising. It is important to take care of your health, and exercising will reduce stress.

- Stay active in your baby's care; give him a bath, put her to sleep. Notice how you feel after you have done these.

The Seventh Month of Fatherhood

There are many roles we play in life. None is more important than being a parent. No matter what job you do or career you have, believe it or not, you are not irreplaceable. But as a father and a husband your "role" is unique and one-of-a-kind.

As men, we are raised to believe that our jobs are the greatest contribution we can make in life. As young boys we are taught that competition and winning are the way we define our self-worth. Relationships, caring for others, those are the things girls do. Being autonomous and independent, not needing anyone, that is how to "be a man."

Being committed to one's family is not an easy task. It takes great courage to understand the needs of others as well as your own. It is not possible to remain complacent as the new responsibilities of fatherhood push us to greater depths of caring and attachment and the feelings of responsibility increase. We can choose to flee. We can abandon our families either physically or emotionally. Or, we can try to understand that our new role as a father calls us to develop another side of our nature. We need to uncover our ability to value the day to day routines of family life that are rooted in our relationships with our partners and children.

It is not just a sentimental thought that fathers are needed by their children. Current research shows that fathers play an important role in the development of their children. Both boys and girls show significantly better academic and social development based on the amount of time their fathers are involved in their daily lives.

It is a life skill to balance family life and work demands. It takes time to understand both your own needs and those of your baby and wife. In the seventh month of parenthood you can begin to notice how much effort it takes to be there as a dad. You've probably had more than a few sleep-deprived nights under your belt by now. Someone, your baby, you or your wife has been sick at least once. Sorting out the chores, the checkbook and trying to find a few minutes for you are all challenges faced by new fathers. Just as your baby continues to grow and develop so do you. In the seventh month of fatherhood your patience should be tested! Be kind and understanding to yourself. Know that it will take time to develop the patience you need to manage all the new changes you are still encountering as you grow and develop as a father.

Here are a few practical tips that new dads have shared with me to get the most out of your seventh month of fatherhood.

For your baby:

- Mobility in every form is foremost now. Watch to see how your baby tosses and turns, pushes with his arms and tries to move around.

- He may even be able to hold a bottle.

- Babies at this age like to watch things fall.

For your wife/partner:

- With your wife, put your baby on a blanket and watch her "do her thing." Talk about how your baby is become more active and interested in the world around him.

- Find a Sunday morning to go out to breakfast and have a leisurely time together.

- Find a babysitter so you can be alone for at least 2 hours.

For yourself:

- Walk around your block by yourself. Think about how your father was a parent at seven months.

- What would you like to do different from your dad as a father? In what ways would you like to be a parent like your dad?

- If you have a brother who has children, call him and ask him what he has enjoyed and what he has struggled with as a dad.

The Eighth Month of Fatherhood

In the eighth month of fatherhood you begin to notice that your baby interacts much more with you. He can recognize you and may even begin to show excitement when the two of you are together. You may be gaining more confidence in understanding what her crying is trying to tell you.

At eight months your baby may be more adventurous and want to crawl or reach for things that may be dangerous. Start keeping a closer eye on him. You may find you may feel more adventurous too, and willing to attempt longer days at the park or even a longer car ride with her to visit friends.

Babies grow and develop on different time tables. At eight months some are just starting to be more mobile while others are beginning to hold on to the furniture and "cruise" around, maybe even trying to walk. Dads also develop on their own unique timetable. While some dads can go it alone and feel totally competent with their baby, others still need to get an agenda or list of things to watch for from their spouse. Since we as men are "trained" to be independent we often won't ask for help from our wives or reject what they may share with us about parenting.

The research on parenting shows that whoever, mom or dad, spends the most time with their baby will become sensitive to the baby's needs. If that is the mother then we as fathers have to be open to learning from what they have observed and value their suggestions. Too often as men and fathers we feel defensive about getting advice or help. We need to know we can't be expected to know how to do everything. Allow yourself to work as a team with your partner on this adventure as parents. Teamwork is the key to getting through this first year.

At eight months you recognize how time-consuming it is to have a baby. Making plans or arrangements with friends means considering what is happening with your baby. Dinner plans or outings are organized around naps and feedings. Sometimes it may feel like your life is not your own, that all the spontaneity in life is gone. Be aware that becoming a family, especially at this stage, means staying flexible. The loss of spontaneity in your life is real. Learn to be flexible and open to the new routines of being a family. Just "letting go" can lead to deep satisfaction and fulfillment. As I have mentioned so often… be patient with yourself and your life, fatherhood will bring to you a feeling of contentment that comes from meeting one of life's great challenges!

Here are a few practical tips that new dads have shared with me to get the most out of your eighth month of fatherhood.

For your baby:

- Waving, banging and throwing toys is what this month brings. Get plastic nested cups for him to play with. Give her a spoon and cup for mealtimes. Continue to feed him, but allow him to do so as he is able.
- He may enjoy seeing himself in a mirror.

For your wife/partner:

- Talk with your wife about a weekend family day. On that day make no plans but just for the three of you to be together.
- Talk with your partner about what you feel are the biggest adjustments you have each had to make as parents.

For yourself:

- Are there one or two friends that you haven't talked with in a while? Call them up and let them know how having a young baby makes "free" time or "hanging-out" very difficult. Reassure them that you are still their friend and ask them to understand that being a father is a big adjustment.
- Ask your father if he remembers what the first year of parenthood was like for him and your mom.

The Ninth Month of Fatherhood

In the ninth month of fatherhood you can begin to notice the routines you and your wife have developed. Who is the one most responsible for the baby's needs and who takes care of the financial matters? Most couples begin parenthood hoping to be equal partners in both work and family life, but it seldom works out that way. Usually at nine months you begin to feel that you have assigned roles.

This is an important time to talk with your wife about your parenting partnership. Is she feeling that you are contributing your fair share to home and baby? Is she aware of the stress you are encountering trying to balance work and family responsibilities? Have you drifted toward the stereotype that men work and women care for the babies? If you are both working is she still responsible for most of the childcare arrangements?

The styles we develop as parents are not as deliberate as we may think. The families we come from and the societies we live in create an "atmosphere" for how we should "be" as parents. As you discuss your roles as parents, try to understand how the families you grew up in and what your jobs need from you, influence your parenting relationship.

Fathering has undergone several role changes over the last hundred years. Being a dad is not a role that is well defined or that has been constant over time. At the turn of the century the father's role in the family was that of the moral authority. Teaching children to read or be "educated" was the father's responsibility. Learning to read usually was directed at learning to read the bible. Being a good father meant raising moral children. If your children attended church and knew the bible you had fulfilled your fatherly duties.

The role of the "breadwinner" father followed as we moved from a rural, agricultural society to a city-centered industrial economy. In the industrial society, the good father was one who was successful financially and provided a house, a car; all the material needs for his wife and children.

In the mid 1970s the role of fatherhood again began to change. The role of fatherhood today has begun to include an emotionally supportive father. As women have dual roles of career and motherhood, fathers have also needed to adapt to the changing role of the family. In our modern society, in 85% of families find it a necessity for both parents to work. This has led to fathers needing to be more involved in childcare.

For many men it is more than the family "need" that they are involved in the early years of their children's lives. The men I have interviewed over the last ten years usually describe the desire and personal importance they find in being involved in their children's lives. In recent studies men have expressed the desire to forgo career advancement for more time with their wife and children, especially in the early years of family life. In this ninth month of fatherhood think about what kind of balance between work and family life you would like to have. What is really important at this time in your life and the life of your family?

Here are a few practical tips that new dads have shared with me to get the most out of your ninth month of fatherhood.

For your baby:

- Try teaching your baby to play pat-a-cake. He may begin to make attempts at feeding himself.   See if he likes to beat on a drum?

- Point to her eyes, nose etc., and name them for her.

For your wife/partner:

- Talk with your wife about the material in this chapter. Discuss how your role as parents is evolving.

- What do you like most about how your wife as a mother? Ask her what she appreciates most about you as a father.

For yourself:

- Take a look at your body in the mirror. Are you taking care of yourself? Think about your diet and all the new needs in life. How do you make time for taking care of yourself?

- Find a friend to go for a walk with once a month.

The Tenth Month of Fatherhood

At ten months your baby can begin to make the sounds for "mama" and "papa." This is an exciting time for both you and your baby. The routines of life may be a bit less chaotic and you may find that you can begin to try and plan a few outings. As a dad, dealing with the unpredictable aspects of the early years of parenting can test your patience. I like to view this period as a chance to learn what really being patient means. As you make plans for the day or the weekend and then find you have to make adjustments, you don't get a good night sleep, your baby has a tooth that is coming in or his first cold; how can you make adjustments and be flexible with your plans?

I remember how happy I would be when our son slept two nights in a row without waking up. I thought, finally we would get back to having a normal night's sleep. It seemed just when I thought we had a "routine" established... I would find the next night all would change! Throughout the first year I would be looking for a routine, yet it seemed the only constant was change. At times I really felt as if I was in a sleep-deprivation experiment. I did find it helpful to talk to my wife about taking turns on certain nights so one of us could get a good night's sleep or at least sleep-in, in the morning.

We are "trained" as men to be "in control." I have never felt as helpless to have a crying baby, which no matter what I did, I could not get to calm down. I think if your wife is breast feeding this can make it difficult for you. Often you know exactly what he needs to calm down, but don't have it! If you haven't integrated bottle feedings talk with your wife about the possibilities. Could she express breast milk and you give it to your baby in a bottle? Talk with your pediatrician about what kind of foods your baby can eat now. Get involved in the feedings. When you find you can respond to your child's need for food or to help her get to sleep, it dramatically improves your satisfaction and confidence as a father.

It is never too late, especially at ten months, to change your routine and find a more satisfying way to work on being a father. If you are feeling distant or removed from your wife or child, don't despair, there are many opportunities to find ways to feel a part of your family's rhythm.

Here are a few practical tips that new dads have shared with me to get the most out of your Tenth month of fatherhood.

For your baby:

- Imitate sounds for your baby. See if he can pull himself to standing position holding on to your fingers.

- Get her a cloth book. Let her hear a clock and say "tick tock."

For your wife/partner:

- Take turns "sleeping-in" to try and keep up on your rest.

- Discuss bed time and morning routines for you and your baby. Find a way that both you and your partner can be interchangeable in meeting your baby's needs.

For yourself:

- See if you can have a routine for just you and your baby. Perhaps it is a weekly walk or perhaps you can be sure that one feeding or bath is exclusively yours to do.

- Find another father whom you can share a weekly activity with-him, you and your kids. Keep it simple, a walk to the park or to get a coffee.

The Eleventh Month of Fatherhood

In your eleventh month of fatherhood it is probably hard to remember what life was like without your baby! Your life as a family and a father may now be the center of all your decisions and day-to-day activity. Your baby continues to grow into the world around him. There is a good chance he is beginning to stand and even cruise or trying to walk. Your baby's mobility is accompanied by your need to keep a closer eye on him. As he explores the world around him, he will find things and put them directly into his mouth.

Now is a good time to reflect on how being a father has affected every aspect of your life. Be courageous and think about both the positives and negatives about being a dad. The dads I have worked with in my groups feel that the change in sexuality in their relationship is the most profound change in their first year of parenting. The redefinition of the sexuality for a couple may take you into a more intimate relationship with each other even though the sexuality may be less.

For us as men intimacy is defined in terms of our sexuality. If you can begin to talk about how you feel about the change in your sexuality with your wife a new dimension in your relationship can begin. In our culture, talking about sex is very difficult for many men. If you can begin to discuss sex, it can often lead to a greater depth of communication in many other matters.

Since your baby was born you have had a constant stream of adjustments to make. There is no handbook for fatherhood. Our training as dads is "on the job." We often don't even know till months later why or how we got through some of those early months of fatherhood. At eleven months we are coming up for a little air, and can look back and see that "being there" for our wife and child has been one of our greatest challenges!

I encourage you to talk with your partner about what your experience has been like. Perhaps you are feeling lonely for your wife's attention and affection. Many dads see what a great mom their wife is and how responsive she can be to her baby's needs and wish their wife were more responsive to them. You may need to make time to see if you and your wife can quit being parents for a few hours and be a couple again.

Moving back into "couple's relationship" is the task of the eleventh month of fatherhood. You have defined yourselves around your child's needs and now it is important to begin to look at your relationship, not just as parents but as partners too. See if you can take the lead and ask your wife/partner how she wants the two of you to grow as a couple as you approach your first year of parenting.

Here are a few practical tips that new dads have shared with me to get the most out of your eleventh month of fatherhood.

For your baby:

- Your baby will probably enjoy being danced about and sung too. She will enjoy watching other kids play.

- Get her a ball and other rolling toys. Stacking toys are a good bet at this time.

For your wife/partner:

- Ask your partner how she feels your relationship should develop as you approach your first year of parenthood. Be specific about your needs for sex, time for yourself, time to be a couple. Remember it is difficult to balance all the competing needs of being partners, being a family, and working.

- See if you and your wife can find a weekly activity to do together. Something that you can continue over time and that you both look forward to.

For yourself:

- Write a list, just for yourself, of the positive and negative feelings about your first eleven months of fatherhood. Allow yourself permission to see that all the changes you have gone through have not been easy.

- Begin to think about you baby's first birthday and what friends you want to be there for you!

The Twelfth Month of Fatherhood

Congratulations, you have been a father for one year now! I would encourage you to see that your baby's first birthday is as much a celebration for you and your wife as for him/her. The first year of fatherhood is the most profound change you have gone through as a man. There have been many changes that you, your wife, and baby have gone through over this last year. Our culture does not make much time for us to make all the adjustments we are faced with after our babies are born. As you have read these chapters I hope you have been able to use the suggestions included to make your transition to fatherhood and parenthood less stressful.

Each family, and each father, has to find ways to make family life meaningful. Although we all like to think that in America, family comes first, I am sure over the last year you have seen how difficult it has been to balance family and work responsibilities. Again, our social structure does not allow us the time or economic support that might help make the transition to parenthood a little easier. I hope in the suggested discussions you may have had with your wife you found a way to create what you needed for yourself and your family.

There is no greater contribution that a man can make than preparing his children to find their way in the world. All our training in fatherhood is pretty much on the job; I hope you have noticed that you have grown as much as your baby has over the first year.

I want to continue to encourage you to find what works uniquely for you and your family. There is no "blueprint" for how to be a family. Each family and each father needs to examine what meets their needs. Perhaps you have become a stay-at-home dad and your wife works. Maybe you and your wife are both working and trying to co-parent equally. Maybe in your family you are working full-time, and your wife is at home with the baby. Only you and your wife can decide what is best for the two of you.

This first year has been both survival and experimentation. Take time to decide how you want the next year to be. Try and be realistic; over time, fatherhood and parenting will become easier, but it takes time and tolerance. We as fathers need to understand that the "tolerance for uncertainty" is the coping skill we need to allow the normal changes of fatherhood and family life to unfold.

I have enjoyed sharing this first year of fatherhood with you!

Here are a few last practical tips that new dads have shared with me to get the most out of your twelfth month of fatherhood.

For your baby:

- Notice how your baby may have about three recognizable words. She will like "pop goes the weasel," especially if you help her clap her hands on the "pop."

- Keep up the pat-a-cake practice. Most important, keep talking and singing to your baby.

- The exciting first steps are near or perhaps your little guy is already on his way!

For your wife/partner:

- Keep up "parenting" talks with your partner. Support each other in your roles as father and mother.

- If you find you get stuck and feel too isolated or angry with each other, talk with your pediatrician about seeing a family counselor. Don't be afraid to get some outside help and support if you need it.

For yourself:

- Develop relationships with other fathers and families with whom you can share experience about parenthood or just "hang-out" with.

- Remember to take time for yourself. Exercise and stay healthy and keep up your friendships with other men.

- Find a special way to congratulate yourself on being a father for one year!

Cymbidiums

You are in the back yard hacking away at the cymbidiums
purple straw sunhat and old pale yellow leather gloves
pruning saw in hand

pink, gold and ivory orchids fill our lives
clumped together they push forth their dragon like flowers
at times I think we may live in the Garden of Eden

I watch as you cut the plastic pot
to free the root bound cymbidium
surrounded by the dark potting soil, bark and
a host of red clay pots you perform your surgery

I bring you some cheese, crackers, a few black figs
sustenance for your work
the hours go by,
you are content in your garden

I appreciate living like this
with you
My love

Quotes on Fatherhood

Making the decision to have a child is momentous. It is to decide forever to have your heart go walking around outside your body.

—*Elizabeth Stone*

Always kiss your children goodnight - even if they're already asleep.

—*H. Jackson Brown, Jr.*

When you have brought up kids, there are memories you store directly in your tear ducts.

—*Robert Brault*

Before I got married I had six theories about bringing up children; now I have six children, and no theories.

—*John Wilmot*

It would seem that something which means poverty, disorder and violence every single day should be avoided entirely, but the desire to beget children is a natural urge.

—*Phyllis Diller*

Your children need your presence more than your presents.

—*Jesse Jackson*

It's not only children who grow. Parents do too. As much as we watch to see what our children do with their lives, they are watching us to see what we do with ours. I can't tell my children to reach for the sun. All I can do is reach for it, myself.

—*Joyce Maynard*

Don't worry that children never listen to you; worry that they are always watching you.

—*Robert Fulghum*

Parents often talk about the younger generation as if they didn't have anything to do with it.

—*Haim Ginott*

The trouble with learning to parent on the job is that your child is the teacher.

—*Robert Brault*

It behooves a father to be blameless if he expects his child to be.

—*Homer*

If you have never been hated by your child you have never been a parent.

—*Bette Davis*

It kills you to see them grow up. But I guess it would kill you quicker if they didn't.

—*Barbara Kingsolver*

Diogenes struck the father when the son swore.

—*Robert Burton*

Children are a great comfort in your old age - and they help you reach it faster, too.

—*Lionel Kauffman*

Most of us become parents long before we have stopped being children.

—*Mignon McLaughlin*

If you want children to keep their feet on the ground, put some responsibility on their shoulders.

—*Abigail Van Buren*

The quickest way for a parent to get a child's attention is to sit down and look comfortable.

—*Lane Olinghouse*

If there is anything that we wish to change in the child, we should first examine it and see whether it is not something that could better be changed in ourselves.

—C.G. Jung,

Don't handicap your children by making their lives easy.

—Robert A. Heinlein

Too often we give children answers to remember rather than problems to solve.

—Roger Lewin

Simply having children does not make mothers.

—John A. Shedd

Although there are many trial marriages... there is no such thing as a trial child.

—Gail Sheehy

Children have more need of models than of critics.

—Carolyn Coats

The beauty of "spacing" children many years apart lies in the fact that parents have time to learn the mistakes that were made with the older ones - which permits them to make exactly the opposite mistakes with the younger ones.

—Sydney J. Harris

There are two lasting bequests we can give our children. One is roots. The other is wings.

—Hodding Carter, Jr.

Your children tell you casually years later what it would have killed you with worry to know at the time.

—Mignon McLaughlin

Do not ask that your kids live up to your expectations. Let your kids be who they are, and your expectations will be in breathless pursuit.

—*R. Brault,*

The thing that impresses me most about America is the way parents obey their children.

—*Edward, Duke of Windsor*

The problem with children is that you have to put up with their parents.

—*Charles DeLint*

Sing out loud in the car even, or especially, if it embarrasses your children.

—*Marilyn Penland*

My mom used to say it doesn't matter how many kids you have... because one kid'll take up 100% of your time so more kids can't possibly take up more than 100% of your time.

—*Karen Brown*

Children aren't happy with nothing to ignore, and that's what parents were created for.

—*Ogden Nash*

Each day of our lives we make deposits in the memory banks of our children.

—*Charles R. Swindoll*

How pleasant it is for a father to sit at his child's board. It is like an aged man reclining under the shadow of an oak which he has planted.

—*Walter Scott*

You will always be your child's favorite toy.

—*Vicki Lansky*

What a child doesn't receive he can seldom later give.

—*P.D. James*

There is a strong chance that siblings who turn out well were hassled by the same parents.

—*R. Brault*

If your children spend most of their time in other people's houses, you're lucky; if they all congregate at your house, you're blessed.

—*Mignon McLaughlin*

If you want your children to improve, let them overhear the nice things you say about them to others.

—*Haim Ginott*

Give me the life of the boy whose mother is nurse, seamstress, washer-woman, cook, teacher, angel, and saint, all in one, and whose father is guide, exemplar, and friend. No servants to come between. These are the boys who are born to the best fortune.

—*Andrew Carnegie*

Now the thing about having a baby-and I can't be the first person to have noticed this-is that thereafter you have it.

—*Jean Kerr*

Children begin by loving their parents; as they grow older they judge them; sometimes they forgive them.

—*Oscar Wilde*

There is only one pretty child in the world, and every mother has it.

—*Chinese Proverb*

Never raise your hand to your kids. It leaves your groin unprotected.

—*Red Buttons*

Kids spell love T-I-M-E.

—*John Crudele*

There may be some doubt as to who are the best people to have charge of children, but there can be no doubt that parents are the worst.

—*George Bernard Shaw*

Because of their size, parents may be difficult to discipline properly.

—*P. J. O'Rourke*

A parent who has never apologized to his children is a monster. If he's always apologizing, his children are monsters.

—*Mignon McLaughlin*

As parents, we guide by our unspoken example. It is only when we're talking to them that our kids aren't listening.

—*R. Brault*

Mother Nature is wonderful. Children get too old for piggy-back rides just about the same time they get too heavy for them.

—*Author Unknown*

The guys who fear becoming fathers don't understand that fathering is not something perfect men do, but something that perfects the man. The end product of child raising is not the child but the parent.

—*Frank Pittman*

If nature had arranged that husbands and wives should have children alternatively, there would never be more than three in a family.

—*Lawrence Housman*

Parenthood is the passing of a baton, followed by a lifelong disagreement as to who dropped it.

—*R. Brault,*

I don't believe professional athletes should be role models. I believe parents should be role models.... It's not like it was when I was growing up. My mom and my grandmother told me how it was going to be. If I didn't like it, they said, "Don't let the door hit you in the ass on your way out."

Parents have to take better control.

—*Charles Barkley*

The child supplies the power but the parents have to do the steering.

—*Benjamin Spock*

Mother Nature, in her infinite wisdom, has instilled within each of us a powerful biological instinct to reproduce; this is her way of assuring that the human race, come what may, will never have any disposable income.

—*Dave Barry*

Having babies is fun, but babies grow up into people.

—*M*A*S*H, Colonel Potter,*

My mother protected me from the world and my father threatened me with it.

—*Quentin Crisp*

When my kids become wild and unruly, I use a nice, safe playpen. When they're finished, I climb out.

—*Erma Bombeck*

I love to play hide and seek with my kid, but some days my goal is to find a hiding place where he can't find me until after high school.

—*Author Unknown*

The hardest part of raising a child is teaching them to ride bicycles. A shaky child on a bicycle for the first time needs both support and freedom. The realization that this is what the child will always need can hit hard.

—*Sloan Wilson*

You don't have to deserve your mother's love. You have to deserve your father's. He is more particular.... The father is always a Republican towards his son, and his mother's always a Democrat.

—*Robert Frost*

Labor Day is a glorious holiday because your child will be going back to school the next day. It would have been called Independence Day, but that name was already taken.

—*Bill Dodds*

If I had my child to raise all over again,
I'd build self-esteem first, and the house later.
I'd finger-paint more, and point the finger less.
I would do less correcting and more connecting.
I'd take my eyes off my watch, and watch with my eyes.
I'd take more hikes and fly more kites.
I'd stop playing serious, and seriously play.
I would run through more fields and gaze at more stars.
I'd do more hugging and less tugging.

—*Diane Loomans*

Most American children suffer too much mother and too little father.

—*Gloria Steinem*

Good, honest, hardheaded character is a function of the home. If the proper seed is sown there and properly nourished for a few years, it will not be easy for that plant to be uprooted.

—*George A. Dorsey*

Hot dogs always seem better out than at home; so do French-fried potatoes; so do your children.

—*Mignon McLaughlin*

As a child my family's menu consisted of two choices: take it, or leave it.

—*Buddy Hackett*

Whenever I held my newborn baby in my arms, I used to think that what I said and did to him could have an influence not only on him but on all whom he met, not only for a day or a month or a year, but for all eternity —a very challenging and exciting thought for a mother.

—*Rose Kennedy*

Was there ever a grandparent, bushed after a day of minding noisy youngsters, who hasn't felt the Lord knew what He was doing when He gave little children to young people?

—*Joe E. Wells*

Ma-ma does everything for the baby, who responds by saying Da-da first.

—*Mignon McLaughlin*

Insanity is hereditary—you get it from your kids.

—*Sam Levenson*

It is not a bad thing that children should occasionally, and politely, put parents in their place.

—*Colette, My Mother's House, 1922*

Humans are the only animals that have children on purpose with the exception of guppies, who like to eat theirs.

—*P.J. O'Rourke*

Likely as not, the child you can do the least with will do the most to make you proud.

—*Mignon McLaughlin*

The one thing children wear out faster than shoes is parents.

—*John J. Plomp*

You see much more of your children once they leave home.

—*Lucille Ball*

Raising children is like making biscuits: it is as easy to raise a big batch as one, while you have your hands in the dough.

—*E.W. Howe*

A young lady is a female child who has just done something dreadful.

—*Judith Martin*

Parenting is a stage of life's journey where the milestones come about every fifty feet.

—*R. Brault,*

Children are natural mimics who act like their parents despite every effort to teach them good manners.

—*Author Unknown*

The secret of dealing successfully with a child is not to be its parent.

—*Mell Lazarus*

No matter how calmly you try to referee, parenting will eventually produce bizarre behavior, and I'm not talking about the kids.

—*Bill Cosby*

The ideal home: big enough for you to hear the children, but not very well.

—*Mignon McLaughlin*

Parenthood is a lot easier to get into than out of.

—*Bruce Lansky*

Conscience is less an inner voice than the memory of a mother's glance.

—*Robert Brault,*

Character is largely caught, and the father and the home should be the great sources of character infection.

—*Frank H. Cheley*

When you teach your son, you teach your son's son.

—*The Talmud*

A lot of parents pack up their troubles and send them off to summer camp.

—*Raymond Duncan*

Being a child at home alone in the summer is a high-risk occupation. If you call your mother at work thirteen times an hour, she can hurt you.

—*Erma Bombeck*

Always end the name of your child with a vowel, so that when you yell, the name will carry.

—Bill Cosby

My father used to play with my brother and me in the yard. Mother would come out and say, "You're tearing up the grass." "We're not raising grass," Dad would reply. "We're raising boys."

—Harmon Killebrew

He didn't tell me how to live; he lived, and let me watch him do it.

—Clarence Budington Kelland

A truly rich man is one whose children run into his arms when his hands are empty.

—Author Unknown

Father!—to God himself we cannot give a holier name.

—William Wordsworth

Love and fear. Everything the father of a family says must inspire one or the other.

—Joseph Joubert

One father is more than a hundred Schoolmasters.

—George Herbert

Blessed indeed is the man who hears many gentle voices call him father!

—Lydia M. Child, Philothea: A Romance, 1836

A father is always making his baby into a little woman. And when she is a woman he turns her back again.

—Enid Bagnold

Sometimes the poorest man leaves his children the richest inheritance.

—Ruth E. Renkel

A father carries pictures where his money used to be.

—Author Unknown

The father who would taste the essence of his fatherhood must turn back from the plane of his experience, take with him the fruits of his journey and begin again beside his child, marching step by step over the same old road.

—Angelo Patri

It is much easier to become a father than to be one.

—Kent Nerburn

The words that a father speaks to his children in the privacy of home are not heard by the world, but, as in whispering-galleries, they are clearly heard at the end and by posterity.

—Jean Paul Richter

Any man can be a father. It takes someone special to be a dad.

—Author Unknown

I love my father as the stars - he's a bright shining example and a happy twinkling in my heart.

—Terri Guillemets

Two little girls, on their way home from Sunday school, were solemnly discussing the lesson. "Do you believe there is a devil?" asked one. "No," said the other promptly. "It's like Santa Claus: it's your father."

—Edward F. Murphy

Dad, your guiding hand on my shoulder will remain with me forever.

—Author Unknown

Old as she was, she still missed her daddy sometimes.

—Gloria Naylor

You will find that if you really try to be a father, your child will meet you halfway.

—*R. Brault*

Sherman made the terrible discovery that men make about their fathers sooner or later... that the man before him was not an aging father but a boy, a boy much like himself, a boy who grew up and had a child of his own and, as best he could, out of a sense of duty and, perhaps love, adopted a role called Being a Father so that his child would have something mythical and infinitely important: a Protector, who would keep a lid on all the chaotic and catastrophic possibilities of life.

—*Tom Wolfe, The Bonfire of the Vanities*

Fathers represent another way of looking at life - the possibility of an alternative dialogue.

—*Louise J. Kaplan*

There's something like a line of gold thread running through a man's words when he talks to his daughter, and gradually over the years it gets to be long enough for you to pick up in your hands and weave into a cloth that feels like love itself.

—*John Gregory Brown, Decorations in a Ruined Cemetery, 1994*

There are three stages of a man's life: He believes in Santa Claus, he doesn't believe in Santa Claus, he is Santa Claus.

—*Author Unknown*

Fatherhood is pretending the present you love most is soap-on-a-rope.

—*Bill Cosby*

When I was a boy of fourteen, my father was so ignorant I could hardly stand to have the old man around. But when I got to be twenty-one, I was astonished at how much he had learned in seven years.

—*Author unknown, commonly attributed to Mark Twain*

This is a Love Poem

When the leaves have left the tree bare
this is a love poem
When the tide has ebbed and the gulls stand
stranded
on an old tree lost in the sea
this is still a love poem
When thoughts of death are near and you and I are
alone
this is a love poem
When our children find lives of their own
and you and I are just part of ancient history
this is still a love poem
When all the forgotten family secrets remain hidden
and the dark cloud of shame floats overhead
this is still a love poem
When the weather is overcast and damp
and it is Valentines Day
this is a love poem

for Carolyn, Valentines Day 2011

About the Author

"The birth of a child opens the doorway to discovering the nurturing qualities within us as men. these discoveries not only benefit our children, our partners, and ourselves, but create a new potential for the society we live in." —Bruce Linton

I started the Fathers' Forum in 1986 with the belief that our lives as dads could be more meaningful, vital, interesting and enjoyable if we were prepared to become parents. This means being actively involved in the birth process and learning about the transition to parenthood. I found that bringing dads together to explore the challenging and difficult first year of parenthood made a huge difference about how we experienced fatherhood. Themes about understanding our relationship with our own father and appreciating the value of male friendships have often been the focus of our groups. I have found that through the Fathers' Forum I have been able to educate men on how to develop friendships with other dads and be able to discuss with them feelings about parenting and fatherhood.

For more information about my work with dads visit the Fathers' Forum online at: **www. fathersforum.com**

For over 25 years Dr. Bruce Linton has been facilitating *Dad's Groups for Fathers of Young Children* and teaching a "Becoming a Father" class in Berkeley, California. He is a Licensed Marriage and Family Therapist specializing in working with fathers and couples with young children. Bruce received his Ph.D for his research on 'Men's Development as Fathers from Pregnancy to a Year Post–Partum." In addition to be the founder of the Fathers' Forum programs, he has a private counseling and psychotherapy practice in Berkeley, California.

You can contact Dr. Linton @
1521-A Shattuck Ave. Suite 201
Berkeley, California
USA
510-644-0300
drlinton.com

Made in the USA
San Bernardino, CA
03 February 2014